Successful Adoption

Successful Adoption

A Guide to Finding a Child and Raising a Family

Jacqueline Hornor Plumez

Harmony Books/New York

For parents who have formed their family through adoption.
They have much to teach us about the value of children and the power of love.
And for all those who are trying to make the adoption system more responsive to human needs.

The case histories used in the text are based on research and interviews. The relevant facts are real, but we have changed names and other identifying details to protect the privacy of the individuals. While the book discusses many legal issues, it is not intended to give legal advice.

Inquiries should be addressed to Harmony Books, a division of Crown Publishers, Inc., One Park Avenue, New York, New York 10016.
Harmony Books and colophon are trademarks of Crown Publishers, Inc.

Printed in the United States of America

Published simultaneously in Canada by General Publishing Limited

Designed by Wendy Cohen

Library of Congress Cataloging in Publication Data

Plumez, Jacqueline Hornor.
Successful adoption.

Bibliography: p. 205
Includes index.
1. Adoption—United States. I. Title.
HV875.P59 1982 362.7'34'0973 81-20200
ISBN 0-517-543516 AACR2

10 9 8 7 6 5 4 3 2 1
First Edition

Contents

Preface

The ability to be a good parent has almost nothing to do with the ability to give birth. Many people would make excellent parents, yet cannot conceive. I hope this book makes their search for a child a little easier. Many others give birth at a time when they cannot provide the stable and secure home every child needs, yet feel compelled to try and raise the baby. I hope this book helps them understand adoption is a loving option.

I know people who can give everything to a child except birth. They ache to hold a baby, long to raise a child. Their initial contact with an adoption agency was so discouraging that they never realized they could find a baby to love and never were told how many older children desperately need parents like them.

I have seen child-care institutions where children were simply being stored. At one, the children were so hungry for human contact that they wanted to touch me, sit on my lap and sponge up any affection I could offer.

At another, I met "Bobby," a handsome seven-year-old, who had been taken away from his drug-addicted mother when he was two. Every year at his birthday and Christmas, he waited in vain for her promised visit.

Bobby and his brothers were living in a group home with

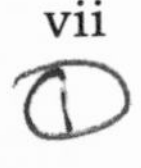

a good reputation and many caring professionals on the staff, but even in the best institution horrors can occur. Bobby was raped by one of the older boys while his brother looked on.

Where do "Bobbys" come from? Consider an urban mental health center where I interviewed for a job. The director said my typical case would be a woman on welfare with two or three unplanned children with whom she could not cope. She would probably be pregnant with another. If married, her husband would either be an alcoholic or in some stage of deserting her. She would be suicidal over her life situation.

I turned down the job, but visions of those women and children heading toward a hopeless future haunted me. I called the director back. Could we develop a program to offer adoption as an option to the pregnant women? Too controversial, he said. These babies could have been given a completely different life through adoption, but unfortunately many eventually grow up in foster care.

I have worked with women who placed their babies for adoption.* Some have a good feeling about what they did. While it was, in part, a sad and wrenching experience, they felt resolved that they had given themselves and their child a chance for a better life, and they knew they had given a priceless gift to a childless couple. Others, like Betty, remained bitter that her family had not helped her keep the baby. Daily, for thirty years, she regretted her decision.

All of these thoughts simmered inside me until I decided to have my second child. It was difficult to get pregnant and I felt the pain and fear of not being able to have the baby I wanted so much. I heard people saying—falsely it turned out—that it would be impossible to adopt.

After my daughter was born, I decided to research the field of adoption to see why so many people suffer in the adoption system, and why it does not serve more adults and children who need it.

I reviewed the research reported in professional journals and found exciting studies showing that adoption is a successful experience for most parents and children. I found other studies of problems that sometimes arise in adoptive families,

*Contrary to popular belief, approximately only 4 percent of all children available for adoption are orphans.

and how they can be avoided. All that was left for me to do was to try and make it more widely available to the public.

I also interviewed many participants in the adoption quadrangle: birth parents, adoptive parents, adoptees and adoption workers. I found social workers, often underpaid, facing human suffering every day. Some had hardened their hearts for self-protection, but most, even after years of work, were still fighting to make people's lives better.

I found dedicated lawyers who arrange independent adoptions. I also found those with questionable reputations and practices. Unfortunately, most of the adoption experts I spoke to treated me with more gentleness and respect when I said I was a writer than when I was taken for a prospective adoptive parent.

The most difficult part of my research was my attempt to discover the most efficient systems people can use to find a child to adopt. I felt like I was cracking a code, and I knew the frustration I was feeling would be a hundred times greater if I was taking these steps to find a child to love.

Last but not least, I found some problems with semantics. I chose to use the pronoun "he" consistently instead of using the awkward "he or she." My desire for a smooth flow of words in no way reflects any lack of feminist sympathy. I refer to social workers as "she" because the vast majority are women.

On the other hand, I feel strongly about the problems of semantics encountered in the adoption quadrangle. Please note that I never refer to the biological parents as the "real" or "natural" parents as some adoption experts do. That would imply that the adoptive parents are unreal or unnatural. Parenthood, *real* parenthood, comes from nurturing and continuing care, not from biology.

I want to thank the many people who openly shared their adoption experiences with me and the many adoption professionals who so willingly shared their research and experiences. The personal stories I include are based on my interviews and on research. I chose to use pseudonyms and occasionally to use composite descriptions.

Special thanks to the following people who helped me by reviewing all or part of the final manuscript: Julian Archie, Patricia Auth, Charlotte Bytner, Elsa Eisenberg, Linda Feieraband, Larry Flink, Laurie Flynn, Jo Guida, Susan Krell, Candace Mueller, Jean Nelson-Erichsen, Bill Pierce, Alan Rosenthal, Andrea Shrednick, Kathe Stojowski, Theasa Tuohy, Andrea Wegener and Susan Weigel. Thanks to the Child Welfare League for use of their excellent library. Thanks to my family and Audrey Bartnet for their support, to Betty Martin and Holcomb Noble for their invaluable help, and to Manuela Soares, my editor, for her unflagging faith in the project.

This book was written in the hope that it could make the adoption process easier for some of the participants caught in the adoption quadrangle.

Introduction

You can adopt if you want to! You can find a child you can love for life. To maneuver through the adoption system successfully, you must be knowledgeable and tenacious: knowledgeable about your own motives for adoption and sure it is right for you; knowledgeable about the various adoption methods and which best suit your needs; and tenacious about following through with your plans until you have your child. This book is being written, in part, because adoption information is not easily found, and tenacity does not come naturally or easily for most people encountering the stress and discouragement engendered by the adoption system.

For people considering adoption, there seems to be no place to go for comprehensive and impartial information regarding all their adoption options. Furthermore, anyone who mentions they are considering adoption these days is often bombarded by a variety of prejudices, misconceptions and falsehoods.

This book will try to help prospective adopters in several ways. Part I provides self-assessment techniques to determine whether or not adoption is right for you and which methods best meet your needs. Part II describes the most efficient way to find a child using each method of adoption. Part III tells what to expect from family life and how to avoid disrupting situations. Finally, Part IV offers suggested ways to change the adoption system, to make it more sensitive and responsive to the needs of all the parties affected by adoption. This last part is included because many of the most effective changes in the system have been made by concerned parents who have formed their family by adoption.

There are those who say it's impossible to adopt today. It is simply not true. It is estimated that there are over 500,000 children in foster care:[1] Up to one third of them are legally free for adoption and waiting for homes. While too many of these children remain hidden in the system, you can adopt others, sometimes within a few months of application. Most of these children have "special needs"; they are of school age, or minority descent, or have problems. People who adopt such children often report that it is so rewarding to turn a homeless child into a loving son or daughter that they adopt another.

What if you only want to adopt a baby? You may be told you will have to wait four or five years. Again, it's just not true. There are agencies in this country that are placing babies within a year of application. There are also lawyers and doctors who arrange independent adoptions in less than a year.

You may be told that all independent adoptions are black-market deals and cost a fortune. Some are, some aren't. There are many reputable lawyers and doctors who act as go-betweens for couples and birth mothers for reasonable fees.

You also have the option to adopt a foreign child. You may be warned that there are no babies available or that they will be diseased. But there are places in the world where adoptable babies languish for need of parents, and they can be screened for health before entering this country.

Prospective adopters are often warned by friends and family that they are asking for trouble. Some warnings are based on the false belief that adoptees come from bad stock and "blood will tell." Others have been influenced by the media, which often give a distorted and negative view of adoption by featuring only adoptees who are troubled and/or searching for their birth parents.

In fact, recent and reputable research shows that adoption is an extremely positive experience for the vast majority of parents and children. Regardless of which type of adoption was studied—baby adoption, older child adoption, foreign adoption, agency adoption or independent adoption—the results all show successful adoptions.

How to judge success? One researcher, Margaret Kornitzer, said that the success of adoption should be judged by whether or not a family relationship is formed.[2] By this criteria almost every adoption is successful.

Another way to judge success is to look at how many adoptive placements terminate before the family becomes legally bound. In only 1 percent of baby adoptive placements do the parents or professionals decide the child should be removed from the home. When the adoptee is over six at the time of placement, 9 percent terminate before adoption.[3] Parents who try to adopt a troubled or handicapped "special needs" child reportedly face a higher chance of failure, but Claudia Jewett, the respected family counselor, adopter and author put the risks in perspective when she said, "One marriage out of two ends in disruption in America. Statistically, it's much safer to adopt a special needs child than it is to get married."[4]

There have been many studies about whether or not adopting is a satisfying experience but few studies of how satisfied biological parents are with their children. The one study available found about 80 percent of biological parents regard their children as a satisfaction.[5] While it is difficult to compare various studies, a similar rate of satisfaction is found when the family is formed by adoption—regardless of whether the adoption is same race, transracial or transcultural.[6]

What about children who are adopted at a later date who have had traumatic early experiences? Aren't parents asking for trouble if they adopt such children? Alfred Kadushin, respected social worker and researcher, studied over ninety children who had been removed from their biological homes because of abuse and neglect, kept in foster care for over a year, and then adopted at an average age of five. He concluded, "The early lives of these children who spent their most impressionable years under conditions of poverty, inadequately housed, with alcoholic, promiscuous parents who frequently neglected them, sometimes abused them, and only rarely offered them the loving care prerequisite to wholesome emotional development, make it difficult to explain the generally favorable outcome of these placements."[7] Kadushin interviewed the parents when these children were teen-agers and found that only 16 percent expressed more dissatisfaction than satisfaction in their parenting experiences.

This is not to imply that adoptive family life is easy for parents. But while it often involves special challenges, as the latter parts of this book will explain, the odds for success for most people who adopt with positive yet realistic expectations, seem at least as good as for any parent.

Is adoption a successful experience for children? Again, there are many ways to judge success. Studies that have compared groups of adopted and nonadopted children find no difference can be found in terms of adjustment, mental health or delinquency rates.[8] In fact, the most comprehensive study, which followed all the children in England born one week in 1958, found that, as a group, the adopted children by all measures of ability and attainment were doing equally or better than all the other children, and far better than those children raised by unwed mothers.[9] The researchers concluded that the desire adopters felt for children and the selection process they had to endure offset any stress growing out of adoption.

Adoption is generally good for the children involved. About 90 percent of adopted babies are born illegitimate.[10] Studies show the homes provided by unwed mothers are often unstable and cannot offer the educational, emotional and financial advantages that most adopters can.[11]

Children, once adopted, become like the parents who raise them. One study of foreign malnourished babies adopted into middle-class American homes found that by grade school the children were above the average height and weight for their own country and were up to average American scholastic standards.[12] Several studies show that IQ tends to rise with adoption.[13] Babies adopted by higher IQ parents tend to grow up with IQ scores that correspond to their parents by adoption.[14] Similarly, the attitudes and morals of adoptees resemble the parents who raised them more than the birth parents. Of course, most adoptees do not come from "bad stock," but even those who do fare well as adoptees. However, the debates continue about nature versus nurture and heredity versus environment—with adoption in the middle.[15]

Any sort of parenting holds risks. There are no guarantees, whether we adopt or give birth, that our children are going to grow up healthy, adjusted and loving us. What does seem clear is that adoption is good for children, and successful and satisfying for parents.

If adoption is so successful, why is it so hard to find a baby? Many blame abortion but this is not an accurate appraisal.

Even with abortion, the number of babies born illegitimately has skyrocketed from 4 percent of total births in 1950 to 17 percent today. There are almost 600,000 illegitimate children born every year in the United States and about 45 percent are born to teen-agers.[16] The number of these babies surrendered for adoption has plummeted, however. In 1971, 13 percent of unwed teen-agers who gave birth chose adoption; by 1978 only 4 percent did.[17] The elimination of Medicaid abortions has not seemed to increase adoption in any appreciable way because of the trend for unwed mothers to keep their babies.

Any girl who gives birth now faces tremendous pressure to keep the baby. Peers and family often tell her it is unnatural and immoral to give away "flesh and blood." As a state adoption official from Minnesota says: "For too many years, birth parents have felt that they had only two choices: abortion or keeping the baby. Public attitudes have to change to give support to birth parents who want to choose adoption."

It is not just public attitudes that must change. Government policy must effectively stress not just sex education, but parenting education so that teen-agers will have a realistic view of the awesome responsibilities of being a good parent. Departments of Social Service must have more incentives to offer adoption as a positive alternative to pregnant teen-agers who are planning to raise their children as single parents in poverty. We must offer as much support to a young woman planning adoption as to a young woman planning to be a single parent.

Social service agencies are in a bind. Criticized for forcing girls into adoption in the past, they now often bend over backward to help birth mothers keep their babies. Even the youngest pregnant girls are informed of their welfare rights, and in some states, a teen-age mother whose parents will not help can have the state keep her baby in foster care for years until she can care for it.

An example of the governmental trend away from adoption lies in a report on teen-age pregnancy prepared by the New York State Department of Social Services for Governor Carey.[18] The report mentions the many problems associated with teen-age child-rearing: health risks to mother and child, failure of mothers to complete their education, high rate of welfare dependency and higher incidences of abuse and neglect. The report lists and recommends many tax-supported services for teen-agers who give birth, but adoption was ignored. In fact, the word was only mentioned once in the whole fifty-page report. Across the country, the situation is similar. Adoption is being ignored as a positive option unwed mothers can consider. New federal laws, however, are trying to limit the extended use of foster care.

Of course, young mothers who can successfully parent should be helped to keep their children, but all too often these girls are not made aware of the difficulties of parenting and the possible benefits of adoption. While many teen-agers make wonderful mothers, most become locked into a life-style of poverty without really knowing what they are getting into.

Any teen-ager who bears a child, especially an illegitimate child, is statistically likely to remain uneducated, unemployed, poor and to raise a large family.[19] The younger the mother, the more likely the problem: Nationwide, 90 percent of girls under sixteen who give birth never complete high school and 60 percent become pregnant again before they reach eighteen.[20]

Teen-age mothers are also prone to locking themselves and their families into a life of welfare dependency: Half of all Aid to Dependent Children (welfare) payments go to families in which the woman gave birth as a teen-ager.[21] More and more unwed children are raising children and assigning themselves to a life of poverty, and our pregnancy counseling programs have been completely ineffective in reversing this trend or in presenting the positive benefits of adoption for mother and child.

The stress of living in poverty and trying to raise a child alone overwhelms many of these girls. Teen-age parents have higher rates of child abuse and neglect.[22] A preliminary study in New York State found 25 percent of teen-agers who are declared emancipated minors (able to live alone with their child supported by welfare) become abuse or neglect cases within the first year.[23] Others voluntarily place their children in foster care. In New York State, for example, 47 percent of the children in foster care were born out of wedlock.[24] Children often get "stuck" in the limbo of foster care and grow up without the permanence they need. Those who come in at the most "adoptable" age—under two years old—spend an average of over seven years in foster care, often lacking any sense of security or stability; some do not even know their parents' names.[25] Many of the children eventually reach the adoption system, but by that time they are often older, troubled and "hard to place."[26]

Adoption can be a heart-wrenching decision for a birth mother, but the future she faces as an unwed mother may be no less heart-wrenching. The assistance we provide must expand to include effectively offering adoption as a choice.

Who are the people who are adopting today, and what sort of assistance do they need? Statistically, over half of all adopters today adopt a child who is related to them—a stepchild, a grandchild or a child whom a sister or cousin cannot parent.[27] Like everyone who adopts, they need a way of assessing whether or not adoption is a good step for them and how to handle the fact of adoption so that it does not cause family problems at a later date. Those who adopt a relative do not face the most difficult task for other adopters—finding the child.

Most who adopt an unrelated child have a genetic or fertility problem. This is such a painful discovery that it is hard to muster the confidence and tenacity one must have to adopt. At first, it seems that no one else has faced such a devastating and cruel twist of fate. Once couples accept a genetic defect, they usually make a positive adjustment to adoption and view it as a better choice than having a baby. Infertile couples may have more trouble initially accepting adoption, especially if they view their fertility problem as shameful. They are often subjected to the myth that fertility problems occur when someone really doesn't want to have a child. Infertility is very rarely psychological.

Of the 2.3 million couples who marry each year, about 15 percent will be unable to conceive a child.[28] New methods of treating fertility problems are being developed all the time, but only about half of the couples with a fertility problem can be helped.[29] For the rest, adoption can provide an equally satisfactory and successful method of having children. This book is designed to help turn the pain of infertility into the purposeful energy necessary for adoption.

Last, but by no means least, there are the prospective adopters who can have and do have children, but find there is room for more. Most of these people are moved to give a home to a child who would otherwise grow up without love and permanence. Even though there is a desperate need for such adopters, they too must be prepared to be tenacious. They can also meet negative attitudes and bureaucratic hassles that will sorely try their loving intentions.

This book is designed to help all those considering adoption develop the attitude they need for success—to come to a secure knowledge within themselves about whether or not adoption is a good option for them, and to know that if they choose to adopt, they can maneuver their way through the adoption system and avoid problems that might be engendered by the adoption itself.

Anyone who blindly enters the world of adoption discovers that it contains a morass of conflicting state laws and a multiplicity of child-placing sources, each with different requirements and different types of available children. There is usually no central source of comprehensive advice or assistance to prospective adopters.

The federal government is planning to collect better statistics, but at this time, no one even knows for sure how many adoptions take place each year (estimated at over 100,000)[30] or how many agencies arrange adoptions (estimated at about 1,500 in the United States).[31] We also do not know how many children are available for adoption, and children often get lost in the foster care system even though there are families who would love to adopt them.

Since there are up to 5 million adoptees[32] in the United States alone, we should be comfortable with adoption by now. There should be no more difficulty explaining adoption to a child than there is revealing any other point of genealogy. Yet telling a child about adoption remains a difficult and controversial subject.

If an adoptee wants more information about his biological heritage or wants to meet his birth parents, this is often seen as a failure on the part of the adoptive family relationship, even though the research does not bear this out.[33] Some adoptees naturally have a higher degree of curiosity than others, and some people are more troubled by unanswered questions. The desire for information about origins is not indicative of the amount of love in a home and almost never results in the adoptive parents being rejected for the biological parents. In fact, studies have shown the opposite—that if an adoptee wants to search for his biological roots and is successful, it usually results in a better relationship between him and his adoptive parents![34] Once questions are answered and fears and distortions are resolved, the adoptee can often appreciate his adoptive home more than ever.

So now you know a little about the forces affecting adoption in America. There are fewer adoptable babies than couples who want to adopt, but thousands of infants are adopted in this country every year. If you want one, you can find a baby either from an American or foreign child-placing source. People do it every day and you can be one of them, but it takes persistence and planning.

More and more people are adopting children who are older than infancy, or ones who have special needs. These prospective parents need a realistic view of what to expect. They also need help so that they do not get discouraged if they meet an unresponsive child welfare system that does not appreciate their offer to give a permanent family to a homeless child in foster care.

Regardless of the method you choose to adopt, be assured that the odds for having a happy family are in your favor. This book is written in the hope of increasing those odds for you. Regardless of what anyone tells you, adoption clearly works. It works because family ties are based far more on consistent love, caring and nurturing than on bloodlines!

Part I

KEYS TO A SUCCESSFUL ADOPTION

1

Should You Adopt?

Sharon and Len were scared to death as they waited to see a social worker at a Florida adoption agency. They were also angry that this woman held their future in her hands.

Sharon and Len worked hard to put each other through college and save enough money for a small home for themselves and their eight-year-old son. When Sharon wanted another baby, they discovered she had developed a problem that might make her infertile. An operation failed to help.

Sharon was devastated. She went through a period of mourning and would become very upset when she saw a pregnant woman or someone pushing a baby carriage. She had dreams about going to a hospital and stealing a baby. When Len saw how much Sharon wanted another child, he suggested they try adoption.

Len and Sharon were lucky. They found an agency that places babies about a year after application, *if* the family is approved. As they sat in the waiting room, they became increasingly tense, worrying about whether or not they would be accepted.

Len and Sharon were also lucky that they had an appointment with Mrs. Byron, an experienced, caring social worker who believes that the adoption application process is a joint effort between social worker and prospective adopters.

"They're looking for our service and we're trying to help them become a family," she says. She does not see herself as a judge, determining who is "worthy" enough to get a baby. Instead she helps couples determine for themselves whether or not adoption is right for their life-style and personalities.

She explained that they would meet together several times to examine whether or not adoption would be a good decision for their family. She asked them a variety of personal questions in an effort to help them decide whether or not to complete their application.

Sharon and Len wished they had known ahead of time what to expect from the agency application interviews (called a home study). This chapter is designed to give you that knowledge, and to let you know the questions you will be asked.

If you can get comfortable with the questions in the privacy of your own home, you will be less anxious or angry when you are asked similar questions by an "adoption expert." If after reading this section you still think you would make a good parent, you probably would! First, some words of caution: Do not assume there is a set of correct answers to memorize, since that would defeat the purpose of genuine self-analysis. Most experienced home study experts can spot a phony, anyway. On the other hand, do not expect a "perfect score." Nearly everyone has some misconceptions and "bad reasons" for wanting a child. If each of us had to get 100 percent on the first try at this chapter, before we could adopt or produce children, there would probably be very few parents in this world.

In a recent poll[1] asking people why they had children, the most frequent responses were

1. I don't know

2. A general liking for children

3. It's instinctive, natural to have children

4. To continue the family name

5. To please other people (usually grandparents).

The only answer that adoption experts feel is an acceptable reason for wanting to have children by adoption is a general liking for children. This poll illustrates the issue that often infuriates prospective adopters: Biological parents do not have to be "approved" to have children; they can cite foolish reasons to have children. Why should adopters have to prove their worth to an agency or private adoption lawyer? Adopters see numerous examples of parents who do not seem worthy of the gift of a child, yet to adopt they have to go through a difficult screening process.

It is normal to feel resentful. One social worker who used to work with adoption applicants said that when she found herself having to apply to adopt, "I felt the whole home study was an invasion of privacy. We feared being judged and rejected. It set up an awful feeling of competition with anyone else who was thinking of adopting." Another adoptive parent, a psychologist, commented, "We had to go through the most excruciating questioning. I was very angry that they were demanding our income tax and bank records to be sure that we could adequately provide for the child, while on the other hand they were helping unwed teen-agers go on welfare to keep their babies."

In many ways it is unfair that prospective adopters have to prove their parenting ability while biological parents don't. One of the reasons that adoptive family life is successful, however, is that adoptive parents must answer the questions that *all* parents should have to consider.

Do they really want to be parents? Are their motives the kind that indicate successful parenting? Do they have the kind of marriage and life-style that will be enhanced by children?

Adoptive parents have to answer other questions unique to their adoptive situation. Have they come to terms with their infertility, so an adoptive child will not serve to remind them of what they believe is their painful inadequacy? Are they sufficiently comfortable with adoption so that they will not engage in any self-fulfilling prophecies about defective genes or "bad blood"? What kind of child can they love as their own?

Unfortunately, everyone who could be an excellent biological parent cannot adjust to the special issues encountered in becoming an adoptive parent. Adoption has most of the benefits and rewards of biological parenting, plus it has unique challenges.

The questions in this chapter and the next will help you determine whether the special challenges presented by adoption are likely to result in the special pleasures successful adopters feel.

Why Do You Want to Have Children?

The answer that indicates successful child-rearing involves both the giving and taking of love. You want to find a special child to share your life. You understand the difficulties involved in helping a child grow and you want to take on these responsibilities. Your life already should be meaningful to you, but a child should add a special depth and meaning to life that cannot be found elsewhere.

Not everyone feels this way and there is nothing wrong with deciding that life can be equally or more fulfilling by devoting one's energy to the arts, business, social life or "good works," instead of to child-rearing. Children take an enormous amount of time, energy and money that many people, if they considered their choices, might rather invest elsewhere.

Do You Have the Kind of Life-Style That Accommodates a Child?

Most adopters have been married (or single) for quite a while and have developed a circle of friends, their own interests and a liking for their freedom. This is natural and good. Children should not be the sole focus of their parents' lives.

On the other hand, a life-style firmly rooted in adult pleasures may be difficult to change for a child. Some children are fitful sleepers and may disturb your sleep for years. All children need a lot of care and attention. If your jobs or interests cannot bend to include plenty of time for a child, the child will feel unloved.

This does not mean that a mother should feel guilty about pursuing her own career. There have yet to be found significant differences between the children of employed women and housewives. (Some agencies, however, will require career women to take at least a temporary leave of absence.) It is important to know whether or not your life-style can readily accommodate the demands of a child and children's activities. You would not want to feel that your child is an unwelcome intrusion on your pleasures.

How Flexible Are You?

Must you have everything quiet, tidy and orderly? Those sweet cuddly babies often grow up to be bundles of energy who get dirty, shout and wrestle around in the living room. While some order must be maintained, it will be very unpleasant for you and your child if you will always be saying "Don't do that!" Some children are by nature passive and/or orderly, but no one can guarantee that a baby will grow up that way. It may be quite contrary to his temperament.

If you adopt an older child, you may be able to specify that you like a child on the quiet, controlled side. But as that child grows more relaxed and sure of being loved, he or she may also grow a bit more rowdy.

Is Your Marriage a Good and Strong Partnership?

Some people decide to have a family in order to save a shaky marriage. It rarely succeeds. As a matter of fact, most partners express more dissatisfaction with a marriage after the birth of a child.[2] This is because children can add a strain to a marriage if they are not mutually wanted and if the couple is not realistic about the effect a child will have on their life-style.

Do you agree on child-rearing practices or do you think you will have fights about rules and regulations; strictness versus permissiveness with children? Are you able to plan together, work out compromises, apologize if things go wrong? Have you been able to work out financial problems and sexual problems? Is there mutual respect between you? Are you so dependent on each other that a child might take away too much of your spouse's attention?

Nobody expects your relationship to be perfect. Social workers who conduct home studies just want to be sure that you are able to solve any marital problems that may arise. Likewise, few agencies expect you to be totally financially secure. They merely want to know that you are not in financial trouble and that you will be able to provide your child with necessities.

What Do You Expect From Your Child?

If you only expect him to try his best in most things and return your love, you will probably be satisfied. If you want him to be very talented or carry out your unfulfilled ambitions, you may well be disappointed. Even the son of a famous musician can turn out to be tone deaf.

Any child is yours to love and enjoy until he is an adult. After that, who knows? You can encourage talent, you can make suggestions, or express your desires, but in the end, each of us must be free to follow his own interests and dreams. Besides, a loose rein can sometimes create the closest ties.

Do You Both Want Children? Do You Both Want to Adopt?

These decisions are so enormous that they are rarely completely equal and mutual. It is quite normal for one person to be more enthusiastic than the other about both parenting and adoption. However, one party should not be very negative about adoption, only agreeing under pressure or to placate the spouse.

Adoption, like all parenting, is most successful when there is a strong family feeling; when both parents take an active interest in the child. It is often destructive to have the wife or husband solely responsible for child-rearing and the one to blame if something goes wrong. An adopted child, like any other, must be "our" child, not "yours" or "mine."

Are You Comfortable With Your Infertility?

It is normal to feel anger, guilt, frustration and even shame upon first discovering one's infertility. Initially, the couple may blame each other or consider finding a fertile partner. If the man is infertile (about one third of cases),[3] he may begin to doubt his masculinity. If the woman is infertile (another one third of cases), she may feel barren and inadequate. If the problem is traced to both, or if the problem cannot be isolated, the couple may have doubts about their relationship.

These are all normal *initial* reactions. Mourning will likely follow. You may grieve over the loss of the child you never had, but the grief and the feelings of inadequacy should pass before you actively consider adoption. If you continue to have a preoccupation with your reproductive problems, you will tend to be either an overprotective or disinterested parent. Or you may be too defensive to help your child if he questions his biological heritage one day.

Both you and your child will probably feel some sadness that you did not give birth to him, but if you are comfortable enough to discuss such shared feelings with your child, it can bring you very close.

One unhealthy reason to adopt is the secret belief that it will cure your infertility. While some women do become pregnant after they adopt, there is no research that proves adoption has any effect on fertility. But more important, if you adopt for this reason you may feel your adopted child is "second best" or you may resent that child if you do not become pregnant.

How do you know if you are comfortable enough with your infertility for adoption? Being able to talk about your infertility to family, close friends or an adoption worker without feeling ashamed or apologetic indicates a healthy attitude.

Who Do You Think Are the Real Parents of an Adopted Child?

Dr. Dorothy Krugman is a psychologist who has worked with many adoption agencies and believes that this question is key to successful adoption. She has found that adoptive parents who raise adjusted children feel they are the real parents. They see the biological parent as a person who has given birth to *their* child.[4]

This sense of "real" parenthood is not automatically achieved, but you probably should sense that you could at least grow to feel this way about a child you adopt.

Are You Comfortable With the Fact That Your Child Will Have Been Born to Another Person?

Studies find that the difference between poorly adjusted and well-adjusted adopted children lies in the comfort their parents felt with adoption and their children's different genetic heritage.[5] The maladjusted children's parents would evade the issue of adoption or would be uncomfortable or negative when talking to their children about their biological heritage. The adjusted children's parents were open and comfortable with the fact that their children were adopted.

This seems to be consistent with Dr. Krugman's theories about "reality." If adoptive parents feel like the real parents, they will not be threatened or defensive about adoption. They will be able to acknowledge the fact that the child was not born to them, but is still truly theirs.

How Do You Feel About the Fact That Your Child Will Probably Have Been Born Illegitimate?

For some people this is a stigma that they cannot forget, for others it is no reflection on the "goodness" of their child. If you are a person who would feel that a child "conceived in sin" will have "bad" tendencies, then you should not adopt a child born to an unwed mother. One woman who was raised by kind but very moralistic parents says she grew up feeling "like a product of sin. I felt I didn't deserve to be."

How Much Importance Do You Place on Heredity and Bloodlines?

Research shows that adoptive parents who are concerned about heredity or the "sexual promiscuity" of birth parents will tend to have problems with their children.[6] Parents who fear the worst from their children often get it.

As documented in the Introduction, recent studies have concluded that adopted children are no more prone to emotional disturbances or delinquency than biological children. Even adopted children whose biological parents were convicted of crimes or engaged in antisocial behavior have no greater statistical chance of being antisocial or criminal than anyone else. If you do fear unknown heredity or assume "blood will tell," you should probably reconsider your decision to adopt. Adopted children usually are worried that they have "bad blood," so parents need to be very reassuring.

David Anderson, a writer and adopter, offers the best advice to all parents.[7] He suggests that when a child is good, you take that as a positive reflection of his biology, your influence and his unique self. When you see the child having problems or being bad, you just assume that your child, like everyone else, has some problems to overcome.

Perhaps you are still unsure about your decision. Read on—by the end of the book you may be more sure. If not, many adoptive parents groups and adoption agencies offer preadoption counseling. On the other hand, you may have decided not to adopt. There are many people who would make good parents of biological children, but would not make good adoptive parents. If this is the case, please be sure to read chapter 3, which discusses biological options you may not have considered.

If you think adoption is right for you, if you love children and have few of the prejudices or insecurities that could cause problems, then the only issues left are what kind of child to adopt and how to find that child.

2

What Kind of Child?

Susan and Paul have been trying to have a baby for years. Each month that passes without a pregnancy brings tears and sadness. Each miscarriage has been an acutely painful experience. Even though Susan might be able to eventually carry a baby to term, they are considering adoption.

Since Paul had some misgivings, they decided to go to an adoptive parents group meeting to learn more about adoption and meet families who have been through the process.

The first person they met told them that it is very hard to adopt a baby in their state, but there are many children with special needs waiting for adoptive homes. She sat them down with a book featuring pictures and descriptions of handicapped, older and retarded children available for adoption.

The descriptions of the abuse and rejection that many of these children experienced had a strong effect on Susan. She wished she could help, but she also felt a sense of revulsion, which made her feel very guilty. Longing for a healthy baby, she could not consider a child with special needs.

Betty and Richard attended the same meeting and looked at the same book, but their reaction was very different. Their three children are teen-agers, but they still had extra love to share. They felt a little too old to get up with midnight feedings. Besides, they thought they would like to adopt a child who would not otherwise have a home. Since this is a very big step—one that alternatively excited and scared them—they came to the meeting to talk to some families who had adopted special needs children. They wanted some straight information about the problems and pleasures involved in such an undertaking.

After looking at the book and talking to adopters, Betty and Richard had a much better feel for the kind of child who would be a welcome addition to their lives. They thought a school-age child would fit into their family, and they might even consider one with a handicap.

Most people who contact adoption agencies are looking for a white, healthy baby, but many come to recognize that there are other kinds of children they can love. Anytime a prospective adopter can broaden the definition of the kind of child he can love, it makes adoption easier. It increases the number of prospective children available and the kinds of adoption resources that can help find such a child. Furthermore, the more flexible one's expectations of a child, the easier child-rearing might be.

For example, if you only want to adopt a baby that will grow into a blue-eyed feminine little girl, you could be in big trouble. Such babies are in short supply, but with enough effort you could find one. The main trouble with such a plan is its inflexibility. Whether you adopt or give birth, the blue eyes of an infant can turn brown. Some little girls are naturally disposed to be tomboys, and it is very hard on everyone if parents try to force a tomboy to be "a little lady." You could be very disappointed, and anytime parents convey perpetual disappointment with their child, the child will probably grow up troubled and troubling. Consider very seriously what kind of child you can love. You must be able to know that child is your own, and you must be prepared to deal with the problems that come with him.

You may be encouraged by some adoption workers to consider a special needs child. If you can love such a child, fine, but do not be pressured into such a decision. Child-rearing should be a joy, *not* a chore, or a mission, a duty or an unwanted responsibility.

Close your eyes and imagine the child you would like to

have. Then think about other types of children that you enjoy. Think about the types of children that turn you off or intimidate you. Imagine yourself parenting a variety of types of children: children from different cultures and countries, children of different ages, children with different handicaps. See how you feel about each imaginary experience.

Do You Keep Coming Back to the Idea of a Baby? Or Can You Imagine Yourself Loving an Older Child?

Many people who initially want a baby discover that an older child might fit into their life-style better. If the prospective parents are older, if they both work and have an active life, a baby could tie them down. Diapers, midnight feedings, formulas to prepare—these chores can bother some people. You might prefer a child that is old enough to share some of your interests and activities.

Older adoptable children have usually had a rough life. They have frequently been neglected, moved from one impermanent home to another, grown to feel that there is something wrong with them or else they would have parents who love them. Some appear fragile and some seem hard, and almost all have a difficult time believing any good fortune will last.

One of the most gratifying experiences for people who adopt older children is helping that child recover from his past troubles; watching and helping him slowly learn to trust himself and his new parents. Some adopters welcome this challenge; others recognize it as an experience they do not want.

When you adopt an older child, you can get an idea about the child's temperament, talents and abilities. Agencies like to arrange meetings between prospective parents and older children so that each can see how the chemistry works. No one expects instant love, just a feeling of liking each other and the belief that love *could* grow. A child's abilities usually increase after adoption, and many of these children blossom when they become part of a family that loves and cares for them. Meeting the child first will give you an idea of his talents and intelligence before you make a commitment to adopt him.

The final advantage of adopting an older child is that they are more available and easier to adopt. In some areas of the country, toddlers and preschoolers are available, but elsewhere they are almost as hard to adopt as infants. In every area of the country children eight years and older are available and in need of loving homes. Just because such children are available and needy does not mean you should feel compelled to adopt one. Remember, the key to successful adoption is to know that you could truly love a child as your daughter or son.

Do You Consistently Want a Child of a Certain Sex?

Many adoption experts say that you should look at such a preference very carefully. It may reveal inflexible expectations that could work against successful parenting. Do you want a boy because he can play baseball with you? What if he grows up with a preference for ballet? No one could accurately predict the character, talents or preferences of your biological children, much less your adopted ones. Odds are, for example, if you take pleasure in playing ball with your son, he will grow up to enjoy it too. But the best attitude is to accept whatever sex and character type fate sends you when you adopt a child.

Does Your Child Have to Look Like You?

If it is extremely important that the child look *very* similar, adoption may not be for you. Read about the biological methods of having a child in chapter 4. These might serve your needs.

Perhaps you just want to have a child of somewhat similar appearance; same race and similar ethnic background. A family of blond Swedish heritage might feel uncomfortable with a black-haired boy of Sicilian background. On the other hand, many would not care. They know that dissimilar looks also occur in biological families and they would not be uncomfortable as short parents raising a tall child or brunets raising a redhead. If you are comfortable, that comfort will be conveyed to your child. If you are uncomfortable, try to find an agency or independent go-between that makes some attempt at physically matching biological and adoptive parents. Matching is no longer done at all agencies.

A more controversial decision involves whether or not

you could love a baby of a different race. Bi-racial and black American babies are harder to place than white babies, and therefore the waiting period is shorter in most areas of the country. However, even though studies have shown transracial adoptions are successful[1] and even though black children may be waiting for homes, if you are white, you might not be allowed to adopt one through some agencies.

In 1972, the National Association of Black Social Workers issued a strong statement against allowing white parents to adopt black children, saying, among other things, that such adoptions rob the child of their racial identity. Similar statements were made regarding Indian children. Many agencies complied although such restrictions may be unconstitutional.[2]

The Child Welfare League's adoption guidelines[3] call for trying to find a same-race home, but do not deny a child a permanent transracial home if a same-race home cannot be found. Still, some agencies will not facilitate any transracial adoptions, while others will.

The important issue for you is whether or not you can love a child of a different race. If you are white, could you see your child's Oriental eyes or black skin as beautiful? Could you give the child a sense of pride in his biological heritage? Could you be comfortable when your child is teased or when adults make cruel comments?

Pearl Buck wrote of her bi-racial adopted daughter, "The first few days, perhaps I did notice when I bathed her that her skin was darker than my own. The first day perhaps I felt strange. But caring for that little body, watching the keen quick mind awaken and develop, enjoying the vigor of the personality, soon made the child my own. Her flesh became my flesh by love, and we are mother and child."[4]

If you know people of different races and have friends among them, you are in a much better position to determine whether you could feel this way about a child. It is also a good idea to meet parents who have adopted transracially and ask for straight, unflinching information about problems they encounter. After this, if you feel you could love a child of another race as your own, you probably could. There are many babies and older children with dark skins available for adoption in this country and in other parts of the world.

How Important Is IQ and Intellectual Achievement?

Sharon, the woman we met in the last chapter applying to a Florida adoption agency, said in an interview, "My biggest worry is that I don't want a slow child. I like bright, energetic children. I don't worry about what the child will look like, but I want him to be bright."

Sharon gave a lot of thought to what sort of personal and family expectations a child would meet. She concluded that she could love a child who, after living with her, turned out to develop at a slower than normal rate, but it was very important to find a child that could be expected to be able to share the family's intellectual interests.

There are families who do not share these needs and expectations. Many families and individuals are choosing to adopt retarded children because intellectual achievement is not as important as other attributes. As one father who adopted two retarded children said, "There is so much sweetness in these children. I really enjoy them. Seeing them learn—even small things—things they would never learn in an institution makes me feel so proud of them and of us."

Can You Accept a Child With "Problems"?

Think for a moment if there are certain handicaps that upset you greatly. Are there any handicaps—blindness, deafness, physical problems, illnesses or emotional problems—you have seen that do not disturb you? Do you have any friends or relatives who have had emotional or physical problems that bothered other people but did not bother you? Would you consider adopting a child with such a problem?

There are many types of handicaps and many degrees of seriousness. Some, like harelips and cleft palates, are rather easily corrected. Many people have discovered that these present no problem for them. Others recoil from the idea of adopting a child with any obvious difficulties.

The DeBolts are a California family who have adopted fourteen special needs children: older children, crippled children and blind children. They have helped each grow into a self-reliant, self-motivated individual because the DeBolts are not intimidated by their children's problems. Mrs. DeBolt has been quoted as saying, "The guilt feelings in parents who've given birth to children with handicaps is very strong. We've been spared that."[5] People like the DeBolts, who believe that the real serious handicaps in life are an inability to laugh or to give, can see what other people call handicaps merely as limitations to be overcome. Not everyone can feel this way. If handicaps intimidate you, do not consider adopting a child with such a problem—and do not feel guilty.

Many of the children waiting in foster care for adoptive homes have physical, intellectual or emotional problems. Do not be tempted to adopt such children merely because they are waiting. Such children present difficult challenges to those who adopt them. Parents who realistically accept such challenges and know they can love a child despite his problems also report they have found special rewards.

Would You Adopt Several Children?

Very often there are sibling groups who are waiting for homes. There are several normal fears when people consider adopting siblings. What if they gang up against me? What if I do not like them equally? The children might unify against their parents occasionally, but parents secure in their role could usually defuse any such tendency. It is also quite normal to love and like different children in different ways. Children who are waiting for homes do not need perfect parents; they merely need someone who can see beyond their problems and admire them as human beings, love them as their own.

If after reading this chapter, you are left with the feeling that you only want to adopt a healthy baby of your own race, do not deviate from that goal. People adopt healthy babies every day and you can be one of them. Such adoptions do not have to be either expensive or illegal.

On the other hand, if you have been able to broaden or redefine the image of the kind of child you can love, your task *will* be easier. The fact that the task may be easier should be one of the benefits, not the reason, for adopting a foreign or special needs child.

Part II

FINDING YOUR CHILD

3

Assessing Your Options

I have never known someone who really wanted to adopt and couldn't find a child. Persistence is the key.

Susan Weigel
Adoption Workshop Leader in Maryland

I tell them to tell everyone they want to adopt . . . to try everything short of putting up a notice in their supermarket. Sooner or later they succeed.

Andrea Shrednick
Infertility Counselor in New York

Frustrated prospective adopters will tell you there are no children available and no place to go for help, but in fact, your problem is somewhat the opposite. There are about 1,500 adoption agencies—probably too many agencies—in the United States, plus hundreds of lawyers and doctors attempting to match the needs of adoptable children and prospective adoptive parents. There are thousands of other sources worldwide. Your problem is not that there are no sources of help, your problem is finding an efficient method of surveying all the appropriate sources that can meet your unique needs.

No children available? Simply not true. There are thousands of healthy American babies adopted each year. The situation you face is that there are more people in the United States and Europe who want to adopt babies than there are infants available. In other countries, however, babies are waiting for homes. Why shouldn't you be one of those people who adopts an American baby, if you want to be? Why shouldn't you adopt a foreign baby you can love? The key is mastering the system and not getting overwhelmed by the difficulties.

No children available in the United States? In New York City alone, in 1979 for example, there were over 6,400 children available for adoption and waiting in foster care.[1] That year there were only 2,000 adoption applicants for those children—and the agencies in charge only got around to screening about half of those applicants.[2] It is *not* that there are no children available, your task is finding a child you can love and finding a child-placing resource that can and will help you.

There are many ways to find a child to adopt. The various methods are described in the next five chapters. This chapter will show you which methods you are eligible to use and which methods will help you find the kind of child you can love. The more methods you try, the greater your chances of finding your child.

If you are only interested in adopting a baby, prepare yourself to make many contacts with adoption resources. It can be difficult to find an adoptable infant these days. Your cause is *not* impossible—thousands of people adopt babies every year—it may mean many phone calls, or a long wait at an agency, or the extra expense of an international or independent adoption. If you only want a white baby, your options get somewhat more reduced because many foreign resources can not serve you. But again, do not be discouraged. Read chapters 5, 7 and 8 on agency, independent and international adoptions, respectively. Also read chapter 4 to make sure you have considered every possible way to have a child that is in some way related to you biologically.

Many agencies will help you immediately if you are interested in a child that is on their waiting list, a child for whom an adoptive home is hard to find. These children usually have one or more of the following characteristics: over eight years old, black, a physical or emotional handicap, below average IQ or part of a sibling group. Such children are described in the adoption field as having "special needs." Chapter 6 tells how you can find the right special needs child for your family and perhaps even get a subsidy to help with his expenses.

Abroad, less severe problems can keep a child on the waiting lists or condemn him to a life in an orphanage or on the streets. Foreign special needs children may merely be older than infancy, or have a minor problem like a cleft palate or polio limp. Foreign adoption is described in chapter 8.

Now that you know which adoption method can help you find the kind of child you want, it is important to consider whether or not you are eligible for each adoption method.

Are You Single?

More and more American adoption agencies are working with single prospective adoptive parents, but they will almost never be willing to place a healthy white baby with a single applicant. Too many couples want such babies, and agencies and unwed mothers who make adoption plans prefer two-parent homes. If, however, you are interested in adopting a child with special needs, most agencies will work with you. Remember, "special needs" usually means school age, black or handicapped.

If you definitely want a baby, independent or foreign adoption may be for you. Many foreign agencies will work with single parents who want to adopt a baby or a slightly older child. But do consider whether you are prepared to assume the many extra burdens that a baby will bring to you as a single parent. For example, the cost and logistics of providing child care while you work is so much greater for a baby than for a school-age child.

Regardless of the adoption method you choose, be prepared to answer questions about your sexual practices and orientation. Most agencies will not expect you to be celibate, merely discreet. Be prepared to show that your life is full enough so that you will not obsessively focus on the child, but not so full that he will be neglected. You will have to show that you can provide adequate child care when he is home and you are working. Plus, you must show that you have friends or relatives of the opposite sex who will take an active interest in your child.

There is a group called the Committee for Single Adoptive Parents that publishes a handbook on single adoptions. They will also provide information on adoption resources. Write:

Committee for Single Adoptive Parents
P.O. Box 4074
Washington, DC 20015

Are You Black or Bi-Racial?

Black singles and couples have avoided agencies in the past fearing rejection by white agency workers. While there still are cases where black adopters are misunderstood and even discriminated against, many agencies are actively trying to recruit black adopters. They will often waive income and age requirements. If prospective black adopters have financial problems, there may also be subsidies available, since black children over the age of two are considered hard to place. Couples who want a black infant will not have a long wait in most areas of the country.

If you want more information about agencies that are trying to recruit black adopters, write or call North American Council on Adoptable Children (NACAC) (see p. 28) or:

Child Welfare League of America
67 Irving Place
New York, NY 10003
(212) 254-7410

They will send you a list of agencies and a newsletter featuring black children waiting for homes.

Are You a Member of Another Racial or Ethnic Group?

You can call or write the Child Welfare League (see above) to determine if there is an agency or group trying to find homes for American babies and children of your racial background. As this book is being written, for example, there is a need for American Indian and Hispanic adopters. Many agencies prefer not to arrange transracial adoptions, and actively try to recruit parents of the same ethnic group as the child.

Internationally, there are children available from many countries. Some countries and agencies give preference to adopters with similar racial or national heritage as the babies.

Are You Over Forty Years Old?

Most American agencies will only place a special needs child with you. They believe that older children fit into the life-style of parents over forty far better than babies do. You will probably only be eligible to adopt a baby who an agency is having trouble placing for some reason.

Foreign agencies, however, often do *not* discriminate against older adopters. Therefore, if you are over forty and want a baby, you will probably have to adopt independently or internationally.

What Is Your Religion?

Some agencies, such as Catholic or Lutheran Social Services, are supported by religious groups. Do not assume that if you are of a different religion, they will not work with you—call and find out. Many agencies require their adopters to be affiliated with some religion, any religion. Some agencies require adopters to at least profess a belief in a higher being or in some moral code, while others do not.

Your state might have laws requiring the adopter and birth parents to have the same religion. Courts have declared such laws unconstitutional, but the practice persists in some areas and at some agencies. If some agencies in your area will not work with you because of your religion, or lack of it, there is still the option of independent and international adoptions.

Do You Have a Physical or Emotional Problem?

Agencies and other reputable sources will have to be convinced that this will not interfere with your ability to parent.

You will have to have a medical exam and usually a letter from your doctor disclosing the severity of your problem. Handicapped people or those with controlled illnesses are often eligible to adopt, so do not assume that an agency will not work with you until you explore the issue.

Are You Divorced?

This is no longer a problem to most adoption sources. You will merely have to show papers to prove your marriage was legally terminated. You will probably be asked about the problems in your former marriage, and your current marital relationship will be explored to determine that it is a stable one.

What Is Your Income?

Agencies no longer insist that adopters prove high incomes. Even low income applicants are welcomed, and subsidies may be provided *if* such adopters are interested in special needs children. Subsidies for special medical expenses are often available to even high income adopters.

In the case of white healthy babies, there are more applicants than infants, so agencies tend to prefer families that can offer both love and some economic advantages. If the baby comes from a birth family that was college oriented, the adoptive family will often be expected to have an income that could expand to help the child through college. If the baby came from a noncollege family, agencies might accept a couple with a lower income. Whatever your income, low or high, agencies will expect you to have no major financial problems.

What Fees Can You Afford?

There will be little or no fee charged if you adopt a baby or older child through a public (tax-supported) agency or in some agencies, like the Family Builders network (see Appendix C), if you adopt a special needs child.

Legal expenses may run several hundred dollars for any adoption; in some states, however, it is reportedly simple for adopters to file the legal papers and handle the court appearances without a lawyer. Your adoptive parents group or local adoption agency can advise you on such matters.

Private or sectarian agencies either charge a set fee, sometimes as high as $5,000, or else charge a fee that varies with the adopters' income. Two examples are given below to give you an idea of the fees you may be charged, but remember that costs vary widely by area, by agency and over time.

One sectarian agency charges an application fee of $50, a $600 fee when the home study is complete and $550 when a child is placed in the home. People who need a home study to adopt internationally or out-of-state may obtain it for the $650 fee.

Another private agency with United Way funding has the following fee scale:

Combined Gross Income	Total Fee
to $10,999	$350
$11,000 to 11,999	500
12,000 to 12,999	700
13,000 to 13,999	900
14,000 to 14,999	1,000
15,000 and over	10 percent of gross income with a maximum fee of $2,500

In the second agency, 10 percent of the fee is collected with the application, 20 percent when the home study is complete, 40 percent when a child is placed in the home, and the remaining 30 percent during placement supervision before the adoption is finalized. This agency, like many others, often reduces the fee for special needs adoptions. They charge a flat fee of $750 for a home study for international adoptions. In states where the law allows licensed social workers to prepare home studies independent of agencies, the fee for a home study for international adoptions is often considerably lower.

Independent adoptions are probably going to cost between $3,000 and $10,000. If the costs get above the $10,000 range, you could be getting into a black-market deal. International adoptions will probably cost at least $4,000 and maybe more if they involve flying to the child's country and staying there for the adoption proceedings.

Many people of moderate means have scraped together or borrowed the money for an international or independent adoption. Regardless of your income, ask your employer if your company provides any adoption fee reimbursement. More and more companies (including IBM and Xerox) that cover obstetric costs for employees are feeling it only fair to cover some adoption costs also.

Whatever method you try, there are techniques that can make your search easier and more productive, but conditions and laws vary across the country, and they change each year. Therefore, it is in your best interest to join an adoptive parents group in your area. These groups consist of parents who have experienced the frustrations of the adoption process. Having reached a successful ending, they now offer support and advice to prospective adopters.

Be aware that some groups favor one method of adoption over another. While some are more oriented to special needs adoptions than baby adoptions and others specialize in foreign adoptions, it is rare to find a hostile reaction no matter what form of adoption you favor. These are people who know how painful it is to want a child and not be able to have one. They are also people who feel the pain of children waiting for loving homes. They can help advise you and support you in your search. To find the parents groups in your area, contact the North American Council on Adoptable Children (NACAC), which provides a link between adoptive parents groups throughout the United States. They publish a directory of their 250 member groups. Order yours from:

NACAC National Office
1346 Connecticut Avenue, Suite 229
Washington, DC 20036

4

Biological Options

It's amazing how many couples do not have a medical consultation prior to applying to adopt a baby.

Charlotte Bytner
Adoption Agency Social Worker in Florida

Adoption by relatives currently represents the majority of total adoptions. The proportion of illegitimate children being adopted by relatives has increased.[1]

Marie Hoeppner
Adoption Researcher in California

Only some of the options in this chapter involve adoption. While adoption is an equally satisfying way to form a family as biology, this chapter encourages you to consider *all* of the biological options. If you want a baby, especially a healthy, white baby, your adoption search may be long and difficult and *all* of the possibilities should be considered.

Some people feel they must have a child that is in some way biologically connected to them. Others who have had continuing doubts about adoption find that their reluctance diminishes once they have assured themselves that it is the only practical way for them to have a family. This chapter lets you review all the ways to have a child who is at least partially related to you. Some of the methods are embroiled in legal, ethical and religious controversy. It is not the purpose of this chapter to recommend any of the methods, but merely to let you know all of the options.

Complete Infertility Treatment

Most prospective adopters have consulted their gynecologist and have had a few tests, but most have not had a complete set of tests conducted by an infertility specialist. Gynecologists are *not* necessarily knowledgeable about infertility. Many do not know when they are dealing with a problem, or do not know some of the newer ways to treat infertility. Often gynecologists may be reluctant to perform tests because they are either expensive, painful or time-consuming. Many patients find such tests invasive and offensive. If the goal is having a baby, however, tests are undoubtedly no more difficult, time-consuming or expensive than adoption.

An infertility counselor who works with clients in the New York Metropolitan area feels strongly that women should read the latest literature about infertility and become very knowledgeable about their infertility problems. She speaks from experience as well as education when she says, "I was being tested for infertility problems, and I told my gynecologist that I wanted to be tested for antibodies (an allergic reaction that can prevent conception). He said, 'Don't be silly, you don't have it.' I had read the journals and I insisted on having myself and my husband tested. It turned out we both had antibodies. We sought an experimental treatment program and the result was a successful pregnancy."

New treatment and detection methods are being discovered all the time. As this book was being written, a new test was announced that showed between 5 and 10 percent of infertile couples are barren because of antibodies.[2] Once detected, the problem may be treated with steroids. Similarly, a study showed that Ritordrine, a drug recently approved by the FDA, is helping many women with a history of miscarriages and premature births.[3] You must try to become knowledgeable about the latest discoveries by reading books and articles on the subject, because even infertility experts might not be aware of the latest advances.

Screen prospective doctors by asking over the phone what they consider to be a complete infertility work-up.

To find a doctor near you who has infertility training, call the nearest *teaching* hospital and ask for their infertility specialist. (Your county medical society can tell you the nearest teaching hospital.) Or, you can write the following organizations for their members in your state:

American Fertility Society
1608 13th Ave. S, Suite 101
Birmingham, AL 35205

Resolve, Inc.
P.O. Box 474
Belmont, MA 02178

Specialists disagree as to what constitutes a complete infertility work-up, but this is one version that is currently used by infertility counselors.

1. Initial meeting to take the history of both husband and wife. A physical exam of the wife is performed. She learns how to take her basal temperature, which she records daily to determine when and if she ovulates. The husband will have his sperm tested to determine if there are problems with his sperm. If so, he will be referred to a urologist for possible treatment.

2. The wife begins taking her temperature daily. The husband begins to wear loose underwear and refrain from taking hot showers and baths prior to intercourse, since sperm cannot live at 98.6 degrees Fahrenheit. (That is why the testes hang from the body.)

3. Disregard old wives' tales such as, "Just relax and everything will come naturally." Or, "Begin adoption proceedings and you'll have one of your own." Some counselors claim that in less than 1 percent of cases, infertility comes from purely psychological causes.

Steps 4 to 14 list tests that should be performed unless there is an understandable, scientific reason why they are unnecessary.

4. Endometrial biopsy from the uterus. This is an important test. It is slightly uncomfortable and is performed late in the menstrual cycle to determine if the ovaries are properly preparing the uterus.

5. Serum progesterone—determines ovulation.

6. Thyroid malfunction tests—easy blood tests determine if thyroid problems are causing miscarriages.

7. Postcoital tests—performed during ovulation and within a few hours of intercourse; determines whether mucus is allowing the sperm to live.

8. Fern test—shows if the mucus is allowing the sperm to travel to the egg.

9. Estrogen index—similar to a Pap test; checks hormonal functioning.

10. Spinbarkeit—simple test for estrogen effect.

11. Microplasm—similar to a Pap, this test reveals a treatable condition that causes miscarriages.

12. Laparoscopy—requires a general anesthetic; tests to see if the ovaries, uterus and tubes are normal.

13. Hysterosalpingography—a somewhat painful test to determine tubal and uterine problems.

14. Immunilogical studies—these tests should be done on the husband's and wife's blood, plus the husband's sperm and wife's cervical mucus to determine if there are any allergic reactions to the sperm that are preventing conception. There is still some controversy about whether or not allergic reactions cause infertility. In some areas of the country there are no labs that can analyze for antibodies. However, samples can be sent to out-of-state labs.

Many of the problems these tests reveal are correctable. If there are incorrectable problems, or if no problem can be identified or if one party has a genetic problem, these are some of the biological options:

Artificial Insemination

This can be done with the husband's sperm or with the sperm of an unknown donor. It is a relatively simple but still controversial procedure performed in the doctor's office, whereby sperm is mechanically placed inside the woman. If the sperm is not the husband's, experts advise the couple to have intercourse several hours after the insemination because it is possible that one of the husband's sperm will penetrate.

There should be some counseling done before artificial insemination to ensure that both parties are aware of their feelings about such a big step. A wife might be reluctant because she would feel only she, not her husband, would be to blame if the baby was unhealthy. On the other hand, some husbands feel like a failure if they cannot provide the sperm to impregnate the wife.

In most cases of artificial insemination, both the husband and the wife feel the baby is "theirs," but it could be beneficial to discuss your feelings with a counselor to help ensure that problems will not crop up in the future. The American Fertility Society or Resolve, Inc., can provide the names of counselors in your area.

Surrogate Parenting

In cases where a wife cannot conceive or carry a baby to term, the husband's sperm can be artificially inseminated into another woman who agrees to bear the child for his wife. Surrogate parenting is embroiled in legal and ethical controversy, but there are those who believe it will become a popular and accepted solution for infertility by the end of the 1980s.

The laws governing surrogate parenting have not been well defined. You will have to find out if surrogates are legal in your state and whether or not it is legal to pay them for their services. Surrogates have been found by advertising or by asking friends and relatives if they would perform such a service. It is necessary that a legal contract be drawn up between the parties, if only to clarify the understanding.

Counseling is necessary for all parties. It is important, legally and psychologically, for everyone involved to discuss their expectations and their feelings openly. If the surrogate has a husband or children, they must be informed. It is important that everyone believe that the surrogate is performing an altruistic service and that they give their support to it.

In cases of successful surrogate parenting, the surrogate reports that she does not feel that she is carrying her own child. She believes she is performing a service more for altruism than money. She feels she is carrying the *couple's* child, not her own. It is very important to have a surrogate who feels this way, since there have been cases of a surrogate refusing to give up custody of the child once it is born. She must give her consent for the child to be adopted by the father and his wife. Depending on the laws in your state, if the surrogate is married, her husband may also have to give his consent.

Egg Transplants

In cases where the wife has blockages that prevent eggs from reaching a place in the body where they can be fertilized, eggs can be inseminated outside the body and then transplanted inside the wife. This allows the wife to carry and deliver her baby. Unfortunately, this method is still experimental and there have been very few babies born using this method. Many experts say that egg transplants will probably not be perfected for wide use until after the 1980s.

Adopting the Child of a Relative

In some places around the world, a relative or friend will gladly bear a child for an infertile couple or will offer the youngest member of a large family for adoption. Adoption among relatives is common in the United States. Usually, the baby has been born to a mother who cannot raise him. There are, however, beginning to be reports of sisters willingly acting as surrogates.

In some families, it would be considered too awkward to adopt the child of a relative. Such an adoption could only take place if the birth parents were dead, and therefore could not create any conflicting loyalty in the family. Other families are very comfortable raising a child whose aunt, for example, is also his birth mother. The success of such adoptions seems to depend on how comfortable the parties are with the arrangement.

If you participate in an adoption among relatives, you will have to be comfortable telling your child about it. Family secrets about adoption can be extremely disturbing to the adoptee. (See chapter 11.) Be prepared to work out an agreement with the birth mother that will cover such matters as visiting rights and what the child is told. Once adoption takes place, you will have all legal rights to the child, and the birth mother will have none. Even though she will have no rights to visit the child without your permission, in actuality it is hard to keep a relative from showing up at your doorstep.

If you can be comfortable with adoption between relatives, be sure to spread the word to every branch of the family tree.

5

Agency Adoptions

Barbara and Ted put their name on a waiting list at a nearby adoption agency two years before they were called to come in for a meeting with a social worker. They met with her several times and answered her many questions about their lives and beliefs. Finally, their application was approved. Six months later, they got an unexpected call that their daughter had been born. The next day they met the baby, and the following day brought her home to love for the rest of their lives.

Janet and Sal were told by every agency they contacted that no more applications were being accepted, but Janet was not about to give up. She called back every month asking to be put on the waiting list. It was almost a year before one agency met her request. She found that by being pleasant, but persistent, she eventually received one of the few babies available through that agency.

The Donaldsons are lucky enough to live in an area where waiting lists at agencies are not large. Even though they had to attend several group meetings with other prospective parents and go through a lengthy home study to be approved by their agency, within eighteen months of application, they had their baby boy. They are encouraging an out-of-state couple who cannot bear children to move to their area, establish residency and adopt.

Most people take their first step toward adoption by calling an agency. Maybe they have heard the agency mentioned by a friend, or maybe they looked under "Adoption Agencies" in the phone book and selected one at random. The choice of agency is made by chance, but the call is far from casual. Most prospective adopters are trembling when they dial.

Will the agency reject me? Will they ask embarrassing questions? Will they have a baby for me? Do I really want to go through with this? Many fears and concerns make calling that first agency one of the hardest things you'll ever do.

Some people never even complete the call. Others get such an unpleasant reaction from their first receptionist that they never even make another. Then there are those adopters who know that the first call is only one step in a process, a process that you can understand and master; a process that will be worth the effort if you get your baby. The purpose of this chapter is to explain that process so that you can go through it with the best chance of success.

The first thing you should know is that there are probably several agencies that serve your area, and each one is different. Conditions and regulations at one agency may be completely opposite from those at another nearby agency. One agency might spend most of its efforts finding homes for special needs children, another might work mostly with babies. Eligibility requirements may vary between agencies. Also, conditions change—a waiting list that is closed one month may be open the next. Even within an agency, one worker can be helpful and pleasant, while another can be curt and harried.

The second thing you should know is that many agencies may be very discouraging. They may tell you they are not accepting applications at this time, and they have no idea when their waiting list will be opened. Be prepared to keep calling all the agencies again and again until you find one that will put you on the waiting list—or until you find your child through another adoption source.

The number of people who initially approach agencies wanting to adopt healthy white babies far exceeds the number of such babies available for adoption. Thousands of people do adopt healthy white babies through agencies every year; the ones who succeed are the ones who keep trying until they have their baby.

Black couples who want healthy black babies may expect an easier time. In many areas of the country, the wait for a black infant is less than a year. There are a few areas of the country, however, where black couples must stay on a waiting list for several years, although in other areas of the country black infants are waiting for homes. Unfortunately, agencies often will not try to help applicants find waiting children in other areas or at agencies other than their own.

Agencies vary in their policy toward transracial adoption (parents of one race adopting a baby of another) or adoption where a bi-racial baby is available. This is discussed further in chapter 6, Special Needs Adoption.

Many agencies do not like to keep long waiting lists, so they are very discouraging to all callers. Some even use this as a test to see how serious prospective adopters are. Does the adopter want a baby enough to keep calling back and pleasantly, but persistently, keep asking for an application or even to be put on a waiting list for an application? Will they keep calling back to be sure they have not been forgotten?

Not all agencies work this way, and there are many people who rightly criticize this method of keeping a small waiting list. Anyone who calls an agency has probably been through a lot of pain. They need and deserve someone who will understand and be helpful instead of rude. But if you are going to be successful, you have to know what to expect.

Some agencies will invite all callers in to a group meeting to explain the local adoption situation. They will describe the children who are waiting for homes. They will help connect parents who only want babies with foreign sources if their agency cannot help.

There are several sources where you can find the names of all the licensed adoption agencies that serve your area. It is probably a good idea to contact each source so that you know you are getting a complete list.

The Child Welfare League of America (67 Irving Place, New York, NY 10003) publishes a list of licensed adoption agencies in the United States. It costs $15, but if you write or call, they will send you a free photocopy of all the adoption agencies in your state.

Also write or call the person in charge of adoption for your state (see Appendix A) and ask for a list of all the adoption agencies serving your area. Be sure to ask if there are any out-of-state agencies licensed to serve your state. (Some of the best agencies, like the Edna Gladney Home in Texas, place babies in several states.) You may have to make several contacts before your state official responds.

The National Committee for Adoption is funded by many of the largest private agencies in the country, including the Gladney Home. Write them for a list of their member agencies and then contact those agencies to see if they serve your area. Write the Committee at:

The National Committee for Adoption
1346 Connecticut Ave., N.W., Suite 326
Washington, DC 20036

On the lists you receive, there will be several kinds of agencies. Public agencies are usually run by county departments of welfare. Some place healthy babies, others are primarily working with special needs children that are wards of the state.

Private agencies are usually nonprofit corporations run by a board of directors. Other agencies are sponsored by church groups. Remember to try church-sponsored agencies even if you belong to a different religion; often they do not discriminate.

Before you call, decide what sort of baby you are looking for. Most white adopters are looking for a white, healthy baby with complete medical and genealogical history known to the agency. Would you be able to be flexible about any of these qualities? For example, if the father was unknown, would that bother you? If the mother had some experience with drugs, would that frighten you? Would you consider a toddler or preschool child? Or a child with a slight medical problem? Or one with a bi-racial heritage?

Such children are not considered very hard to place, and few are waiting for homes, but if you can tell an agency that you will consider a child that may be slightly hard to place, it might make your chances for success a lot better.

The following sequence of events is typical of what you can expect if agencies in your area are accepting applications.

1. Call *all* the agencies that serve your area.

2. You will probably be asked some preliminary questions on the phone: How long have you been married? (Most agencies want you to have been married at least two or three years.) How old are you? (Most agencies place babies with people twenty-one to forty years old.) What sort of child are you looking for?

3. You can ask initial questions like, How long is your waiting list? How many babies do you place each year? What are your fees? Are there any children waiting for adoptive homes? (There may be children with a "problem" that does not seem like a problem to you.)

4. Some agencies will invite you to a group meeting with other prospective adoptive parents. Here they will explain their procedures and give you a realistic idea of the waiting time and eligibility requirements.

5. Request an application, or ask to be put on a waiting list for an application at any agency that seems able to meet your needs. You can apply to more than one agency, but whether or not to reveal this is your decision. It is probably best not to lie to the agency if they ask about applications elsewhere. Tell them you want a baby so much that you felt you had to try all possible sources. Because of the expense and inconvenience, you probably would not want to go through more than one home study.

6. Once you submit your application, you may have to call every month or so to be sure your request for a home study is active. Keep a record of all these calls. Always be pleasant but persistent about pressing your desire for a child and your belief that you could pro-

vide a good and loving home. If months go by, check with the adoption supervisor to see what is happening. You may even wish to stop in, in person, so they will remember you.

7. Join an adoptive parents group or a parents auxiliary of the agency. This will not only give you support during the difficult waiting period, but will show the agency you are serious about adoption.

8. Once a home study is begun, chances are good that you will eventually get your child. A home study is a series of interviews between you and an agency social worker to determine if adoption is right for you. You will be asked many of the same questions you considered in Part I of this book. Try to be relaxed, honest and positive about your desire for a child.

   Good agencies treat a home study as a partnership. They do not try to be hostile or judgmental. Rather, they believe that they are helping *you* decide whether or not to pursue adoption. Rarely do they turn down a couple who seems to have a relatively stable marriage and a strong, mutual desire to become adoptive parents.

   In fact, some of the most progressive agencies are conducting home studies where the parents themselves rate their own acceptability as prospective adopters. They even get to write up their own home study report. Such agencies have found that prospective adopters can accurately assess how suitable adoption is for them if they are guided through thought-provoking exercises by their social workers.

   The social worker may ask difficult questions and may create some stress to see how you handle it. But if you are working with someone who continually treats you as an adversary, ask him about this. If you can't work it out, you can ask the director of the agency to assign you a new social worker. Your social worker should be your partner and your helper—not your opponent.

9. Either before or during the home study, the agency will ask for documents like your birth certificates, marriage license, references from friends, a doctor's examination and verification of your employment. They may ask for financial records. If you have been divorced, you may have to provide the legal papers. Your references and your interviews do not have to prove you are wealthy, only that you do not have any major money problems. You do not have to prove that you would be perfect parents, only that you and your spouse could make a caring parenting team. Your marriage doesn't have to be completely problem-free, but you must show you can work out problems that come up.

10. The social worker will visit you in your home. It will not be a surprise visit, and you need not worry if your home is not impressive. She won't snoop under your bed; she will determine that there is a place for the child to sleep and conditions are reasonably hygienic.

11. The social worker will want to know if the wife will work outside the home. The agency may expect her to give up a career for several years, or at least work part time. Some approve working mothers, but they will expect excellent child-care plans. It is probably safest to say that you will give up your career, at least for a while, to be a mother. Once the adoption is final, you can do whatever suits your needs and life-style. Of course a child needs both parents around much of the time, but studies have found no significant differences between the children of women who work outside the home and full-time mothers, so long as excellent child care is available.

12. The agency will want to know how the immediate family feels about adoption. If grandparents oppose adoption, how will you handle the problem? Most grandparents come to accept a child once they get to know him, but you may have to be prepared to sever

relations with relatives who continue to be hostile to your child or adoption.

13. Once the home study is complete, ask whether or not you have been approved. If your home study results in your application being turned down, you have a right to know why. Some agencies will give you the chance to appeal the decision. Contact the director of the agency and request an appointment, or at least a review, if you feel you have not been judged properly.

Try to be honest with yourself. Did the agency have a valid reason for turning you down? Are you and your marriage stable enough to enjoy a child? Are you really ready to be an accepting and loving parent? Are your expectations of parenthood realistic? If you still want to parent and believe you would enjoy the job, apply to other agencies and try other adoption methods. There are many people who have been rejected by one agency and go on to become happy and successful adoptive parents!

14. If you have been approved, the agency has made a commitment to you and will place a child with you. The only question is how long the wait will be. Some agencies try to match the child to the parents' interests and personalities; other agencies do not.

Ask about the wait. They should be able to give you an estimate. Try to spend time with babies so you will be comfortable with yours. It can be frightening to suddenly be presented with your first child. Get some practice handling crying babies or changing squirmers.

15. Once you get the call that your baby is waiting for you, you will be invited to meet the baby. You will be given a chance to see if you are comfortable with the baby and if you feel positively toward it.

Don't be surprised if you do not feel instant love, but you should feel that you want this baby. If you have reservations, discuss them. No good agency will reject you for this. Perhaps you are just feeling first-parent jitters. That's normal. Perhaps, though, there is something about this baby that does not fit with you. Does he look like a relative you hate? Does his extremely active style clash with your passive one? If there are any problems, now is the time to see if they can be worked out. Most agencies will allow a couple to turn down one baby for good cause and still be offered another. Adopters rarely do this, but it is comforting to know it is possible.

16. The agency may make you wait a day before bringing the baby home, just to be sure you want to adopt. After you bring him home, that baby will be emotionally yours but probably not legally yours for several months. In most states the baby must live with you for six months to a year before the final adoption decree.

During this time, your agency social worker will visit you a few times to see if everything is going well. Most adopters live in fear of these visits, imagining that the baby will be taken away from them if anything "wrong" is discovered. Calling this period of time "probation" fosters these fears. In fact, once the agency gives you a child, they consider that baby yours. You would have to be grossly negligent to have them take the baby away. Your agency social worker will not be looking for problems; she will, instead, want to help you with any difficulties that you, like any new parents, might have with a new baby.

All new parents have fears and lists of questions about their babies. The social worker is there to help. If you are more comfortable asking someone else such questions, find a pediatrician or an adoptive or biological parent who will provide that necessary support.

What if you have not been able to get on an agency waiting list? What if your repeated calls bring nothing but curt refusals? Ask to speak to the director of each agency. Explain your strong desire to adopt and ask if any other agency or method of adoption can be recommended to help you find the kind of child you want.

Contact adoptive parents groups in your area. (See page 28.) Many groups conduct preadoption workshops where they give specific advice about adoption sources, while others are very willing to offer informal advice. Above all, do not be discouraged, there are other ways to adopt than through an agency.

Agencies should be your first option, because they usually offer the least expensive and most reliable method of adoption. However, because fewer and fewer birth mothers are placing their babies with adoption agencies, prospective adoptive parents have to consider other alternatives. Many people adopt babies through independent and foreign sources. Others begin by wanting a baby and end up deciding that an older child is for them. One agency director smiled as she told of a childless couple she met seven years ago when they came wanting a white healthy baby. Now they are the happy but harried parents of seven children ranging in age from fourteen to twenty-two! If you definitely want a baby, and only a baby, however, keep pursuing your dream. It can come true.

6

Special Needs Adoptions

Betty and Richard were the couple we met a few chapters back who initially thought of adopting an older child. Their biological children were teen-agers and they liked being parents. They wanted to share their home with a child who otherwise might grow up with nothing. They were even considering a handicapped child.

After looking through several photo-listing books featuring children waiting for homes, and after participating in several group meetings of prospective special needs parents, they decided they could accept a learning handicap better than a physical one. They adopted their thirteen-year-old son who was labeled retarded. Part of their pleasure has been seeing his progress. Slowly but surely he has begun to learn more than they ever thought possible. He will never go to college, but he can become a self-supporting adult.

Margueritte is a forty-three-year-old black woman with many friends. Despite her work and her interests, she was beginning to feel that life had passed her by. Holidays were especially lonely and made her regret never having children. When a friend at work, a single white woman, adopted a black sixth-grader, Margueritte was shocked—but it got her thinking. Recently she adopted two sisters, one eight and one five.

The girls have not made an easy adjustment, but this Thanksgiving Marguerittte gave genuine and hearty thanks that they had come into her life.

The term "special needs" adoption can mean very different things to different people. In general it refers to the adoption of children for whom agencies have to actively recruit parents. Although babies are not usually considered as having special needs unless they are handicapped, some agencies in some parts of the country do have minority or bi-racial babies waiting for homes. These babies are not strictly considered special needs because they could easily find homes if they were listed on statewide or interstate adoption exchanges, but not all agencies use these exchanges and therefore some healthy babies may be available simply because they are not white.

Most children labeled "special needs" have characteristics that present too great a challenge for the average adopter. The "need" is usually that the child is school-age or of a minority heritage. Some waiting babies and children have serious handicaps. In the past these children were considered unadoptable and destined to grow up in a series of foster care placements. Largely through the pressure of national advocacy groups and adoptive parents groups, more agencies recognize that special needs children can find families to adopt and love them.

What kind of children are we talking about? No one keeps a valid statistical count, although the federal government is planning to do so. A national survey[1] was conducted that found 102,000 children in foster care who were legally free for adoption and another 11,000 who were to be released for adoption. Another 37,000 children were in foster care because their parents were unwilling to care for them, plus another 40,000 because their parents had abandoned them—but there was no plan for adoption on record for these children.

Of the 102,000 free for adoption, 52 percent were free because their parents voluntarily gave up their rights to them, 34 percent had parental rights involuntarily terminated, usually because of abuse or neglect by the parents. The remaining 14 percent were free predominantly because of death of or abandonment by their parents.

Only 9 percent of the children legally free were under one year old. Thirty-one percent were between one and six years old and the rest, 60 percent, were between seven and seventeen years. Sixty-three percent of the children were white, 28 percent black and the remaining children were Hispanic, Indian, Oriental or "other."

An estimate[2] of the characteristics of children free for adoption in New York State reflects other pertinent characteristics of children waiting for homes in other states: two thirds are boys, one third have a below-average IQ and half have some physical, emotional or mental handicap. Handicaps range from minor correctable ailments to severe permanent damage.

Most of these children came into foster care on a "temporary" basis because their parents could not take care of them. The parents were undergoing periods of personal, financial or marital stress. These problems never resolved themselves to a point where the child could rejoin the family. Other children were removed from parents who neglected or abused them. These children have had a sad past. Added to their burdens is the fact that many of them have stayed in the limbo of foster care for years. Every one of these children badly needs love, understanding and the security of a permanent home with parents who care deeply about them.

Adopting one of these children is a big step and a big commitment. Parents who have done it will readily admit they often ask themselves why in the world they did such a foolish thing! But they also speak of the pride they take in their child's accomplishments, of the good feelings they get for providing the chance of a better life and of the love that grows as a homeless child is transformed into a son or daughter.

There are stories of almost miraculous changes in children. Many considered retarded have become average learners. For example, one illiterate eleven-year-old girl was able to function at grade level after three years in an adoptive home. Many withdrawn children learn to laugh and crippled children learn to walk given love, attention and encouragement. You can watch this process in documentary films[3] made about the DeBolt family in California, which has blended six biological children and fourteen special needs children into a cohesive and well-functioning family. The adoptees are of various races and many have serious handicaps like blindness and missing limbs, but each contributes to the family.

Anyone adopting a special needs child must know that such miracles do not always take place. You will have to be able to love and accept the child you adopt if he does not change at all. You will also have to recognize that any child who has been through years of foster care will probably have sustained some mental or emotional damage, if only because the impermanence of the situation engenders insecurity.

Alfred Kadushin, a pioneering researcher who studied children adopted from foster care at an average age of five, was surprised to find that their adjustment was only slightly lower than children adopted at infancy. Estimates of the success of more difficult placements are not so optimistic, however. At least 9 percent of parents and/or children make the heartrending decision for the child to leave the family before adoption is finalized.[4] But for those parents who successfully adopt a special needs child, it is often such a gratifying experience that they go on to adopt another—and in some cases, many. Special needs adoption seems to be addictive.

How to be sure you are one of the successful adopters? Go into it with your eyes open. Talk to other parents who have succeeded and failed. Develop a good idea about the types of special needs that won't overwhelm you. You must have a realistic view of what your child's problems will be and know that you can develop a program to help him grow as strong and independent as possible without pushing him excessively.

Get in touch with your motivations. You can't be considering adoption only out of pity or a desire to prove what a good person you are, but of course compassion and kindness will be part of your decision. Enter adoption with a firm sense of commitment, but remember that it is normal to have strong swings from confidence to panic. Feeling a little confused? That's normal.

The first step out of confusion is to decide what kind of child to adopt. Look through several of the state and regional photo-listing books of children waiting for adoption. Looking at these pictures and reading the descriptions of children will give you a good feel for the kinds of children you can love. These books should be available through adoption agencies or parent support groups in your state. If you have any problem finding them, contact NACAC (see page 28).

Your local adoptive parents group will be able to introduce you to families who have adopted children with special needs. Meeting these children and their parents will help you decide whether or not special needs adoption is for you.

Tell your family and friends what you are considering. Many will probably say you are crazy. How do you hold up under such criticism? As you defend your position and explain your motives, does it strengthen or weaken your resolve? Be honest with yourself. Could you loosen—even sever—family ties or friendships with people who refused to accept your child? Are you too proud to seek professional counseling if problems developed with your child or your family? Many older children need psychological help to cope with emotional damage that took place before you met them. Love is not always enough to cure old wounds.

Older Children

There are some advantages to adopting an older child. He can share activities with you and he often fits easier than a baby into a family where mother works outside the home. You can get to know the child through visits before he comes to live with you. This will give you an idea about whether or not you are temperamentally suited to each other. You will know in advance what some of his strengths and weaknesses are and how he performs in school.

On the other hand, you have to recognize that a child who has been in and out of foster homes is probably, to some degree, a troubled child. He may never have known adults whom he could count on for consistent affection. He may never have had anyone happy to see him when he came home from school or proud of him when he made a small achievement. He will have little self-confidence and many fears. Why should he believe you will love him and stick by him when no one else has?

It would be insensitive to expect that he could change quickly. You will have to be the kind of person who does not panic when he becomes difficult, or when a period of good behavior turns rotten. You will have to deeply disbelieve the doomsayers who claim that a child is irreparably harmed by early experiences. Perhaps most difficult, you will have to be comfortable with his memories and remarks about other parents, good and bad. As one woman who has adopted several older children says, "There is a part of the children that can never be yours."

Children under six are far more easy to place than older children, but also may make a difficult adjustment. A child in the two- to four-year age group finds change difficult and does not have the verbal and intellectual skills to understand what is happening to him. He can't tell you about his fears. He might be passive and depressed, or might throw temper tantrums. You will merely have to stand by and offer reassurance until your child learns to trust.

An older child can communicate better, but you might not like what you hear. He may have learned language that will shock the neighbors, and as all cursers know, obscenity is a hard habit to break. He may also prattle on about how great his biological or foster parents were. He may be listed as hyperactive. If so, be sure you meet a similar child and discover whether or not you will start bouncing off the walls with him.

When an older child comes to you, he will probably look skinny and scruffy. He will probably be clumsier and lack the concentration of other kids his age. His insecurities may come out in lying, stealing or bed-wetting. He may regress and act childish. He will almost certainly test your love with bad behavior at some time or another. He should grow out of many of these problems given the security and permanence of your home, but there are no guarantees.

You will have to stand by him, being tolerant but firm when his behavior gets out of hand. You will have to baby him if he needs it, but help him to grow strong and mature. Most likely you will be rewarded by the pleasure of seeing your child learn to love and trust you. You will know that even if your child does not fully blossom, you have given him a chance for a better future.

Sibling Groups

Many children in foster care have brothers and sisters. Sometimes some siblings are kept by the biological parents, and this can be hurtful to the children who are placed for adoption. Other times all the children are available for adoption.

In some cases where each child needs a lot of individual attention to make up for past deprivation, sibling groups are split up into separate adoptive homes. In other cases, siblings have grown quite attached to one another. The only security they have known has come from their affection for one another. In those cases, adoption workers try to find parents who will accept the whole group.

Often the oldest child has acted as the caretaker and surrogate parent. If he has gained his positive identity from this role, he might not give it up easily. He may also have learned that he must keep his guard up, even against people who appear friendly, to protect the younger ones. It is not unusual for a child like this to regress in age even further than his youngest sibling, when he can finally relax. Then he can grow up again, once he has had his needs for babying met.

Transracial Adoption

The first transracial adoptions to take place in any numbers occurred in the 1950s when Harry Holt, an Oregon farmer, decided to do something about the needs of Korean children orphaned by the war. Ignoring conventional home study practices, he placed thousands of children in the United States, and many adoption experts were shocked by his audacity and his success. In the late fifties, some agencies began offering black infants, previously considered unadoptable, to white applicants. Again, to the surprise of many traditional adoption workers, white parents wanted these children and the adoptions were successful. By the early 1970s over a third of the black children adopted were joining white families.[5] Even with the active recruitment of minority adopters and the acceptance of many white families, there were not—and still are not—enough homes for all the minority children in need of adoptive homes.

In 1972, the National Association of Black Social Workers issued a position paper in vehement opposition to whites adopting blacks. They said that for blacks to survive in our racist society, they had to grow up with a strong racial identity impossible to obtain in white homes. Others have argued that if our racist society is ever to change, it will be through the examples of loving transracial families. Then there are those who assert that children need permanent homes and that racial politics should not keep children in foster care when homes of any color are available.

Because of protests, or because of prejudice, many agencies will not place across racial lines. Many have been creative and insistent in their efforts to recruit black adopters. Unfortunately, prospective black and white adopters feel rebuffed by some agencies, or else are kept on waiting lists while black children wait for homes elsewhere.

The Child Welfare League has issued adoption standards that state that it is preferable to place a child with parents of his own race, and that an agency should actively try to find such parents. However, the standards further state a child "should not have adoption denied or significantly delayed when adoptive parents of other races are available."[6]

In some cases where a child has developed a strong, positive racial identity, his agency should only consider same-race parents. But many youngsters have only vague concepts of race and should not have to wait years in foster care until agencies develop adequate black recruiting methods. Furthermore, it is probably unconstitutional to reject adopters because they do not have the same race or religion as available children.

Should you adopt across racial lines? The answer may lie in other questions. Do you think you could truly call a child of another race "son" or "daughter"? Are you the kind of person who doesn't care much about the opinions of others or can withstand insults? Can you cope with prejudice shown to your child?

One study of transracial adoption found that there are two kinds of white families who adopted black children.[7] One type was a small-town family, church members, who had few black friends. The other type was more socioeconomically successful, lived in an urban area, and had black friends. The researchers seemed almost surprised to report that both types were equally successful adopters, and that "it is possible to adhere to a relatively conventional 'middle American' life-style and yet be relatively free of prejudice in the area of race and have something to offer children whose racial background is different."[8]

These researchers, studying 125 children on the average of seven years after adoption, found that half the children had encountered some form of social cruelty, but it had not harmed their adjustment or their relationships with other children. Half the parents reported some initial opposition from their families to the idea of transracial adoption, but this usually disappeared once the adoption took place.

After interviewing parents and teachers, and giving the children personality tests, they concluded that even though the adoptions took place at a much older age than usual, and even though the families had to contend with the stress of transracial living, there was a 77 percent success rate. Most of the parents described their child-rearing experiences as "extremely satisfying." They felt enriched by their child. If you think you would feel the same way too, you will probably be successful.

Handicaps

Some children waiting for homes have correctable physical problems. They could hear again, see again, walk again or have minor plastic surgery if only they had supportive parents who would secure the necessary help. Other problems such as cerebral palsy, severe retardation and uncorrectable physical problems will never improve much, if at all.

There are also a vast number of children with emotional problems and learning problems who may or may not improve given a loving, permanent home. When adopting children like this, you have to love them as they are and be proud of them even if they never change. You will have to shrug off the incredulous responses you get from some friends, relatives and even an occasional agency worker when you tell them your intention to adopt a handicapped child. You will have to disregard the stares or remarks that some people will make to your son or daughter.

Anyone considering such an adoption should begin by listing the handicaps with which they are comfortable. Find out about the services in your community for people with similar problems. Talk to parents of such children and play with the kids. Get a good, realistic feel for what you are getting into.

You and your family will have to be relaxed with the problem and see it as a limit to be accepted or overcome. You must not tolerate self-pity.

If there are only a few specific handicaps you can accept, few such children may be available and you may have a wait. One man who wanted to adopt a deaf child sent a flyer to all the state adoption officials and adoption exchanges trying to find a healthy deaf child.

Other handicaps are more common in adoptable children. Mentally retarded children, for example, are widely available. Some of these children are so retarded that they will need nursing care forever. Parents have been found for these children—the kind of people who enjoy giving and do not expect much in return. Moderately retarded children can grow up to work in special workshops or under low-pressure conditions. Parents of these children feel the satisfaction of helping a child gain the independence he would probably never have found in foster care.

The majority of children labeled retarded are only mildly affected. The child might never go to college, but will be able to become self-supporting and even hold a responsible job. Some kids labeled retarded are not really so. The stress and unhappiness of their life situation plus their poor schooling causes them to get low scores on their IQ tests. They may never get straight A's, but their problems are neither organic nor permanent. You will probably not be able to tell whether your child can become a normal learner or not. You must be able to accept the child if he never improves on his diagnosed level of learning.

If you are considering adopting a retarded child, your rewards will be the affection they usually freely show. You will be as proud of your child learning to dress himself as another parent would be of a child majoring in physics.

Parents thinking of adopting any sort of handicapped child will have to have a great deal of patience and flexibility. They will have to love to talk to and encourage their child without pushing. They will have to enjoy giving rather than receiving and have the ability to love someone whom many people do not find appealing. If this describes you, there are many children who desperately need your love.

How can you find your child? Be tenacious. You may be

given the impression that there are no children available. In fact, as stated earlier in the chapter, there are probably at least 100,000 children already free and waiting for permanent homes. Yet many remain hidden in the system.

To illustrate this point, here is an example of what happened to prospective adopters in one suburban county—a county that has the reputation of having several good adoption agencies and a caring county administrator of social services. When several people called agencies asking about special needs children, they were rebuffed on the phone or told none were available. A woman who contacted the county about running a column in the local paper featuring waiting children was told there were only 6 in the county. In fact there were 261 children legally free for adoption in foster care.

Why do things like that happen? Some say it is because agencies collect government fees for overseeing children in foster care and would lose their operating funds if "their" children were all placed in adoptive homes. Some say that foster care workers do not believe in the value of or need for adoptive homes for children already in decent foster care. Others say that adoption and foster care professionals are too overloaded and underpaid to be efficient. Often agencies believe that a child should be given lengthy therapy before he is ready for an adoptive home.

Whatever the reason, taxpayers pay up to $30,000[9] per year to keep a child in foster care when he can be adopted. Prospective parents are often treated rudely when they try to adopt, and most important, these children have to spend each day wondering if they will be moved again, feeling the lack of permanence in their lives, and deprived of parents committed to loving them forever. Even loving foster homes cannot provide a child with the security he needs from being a permanent part of a family for life.

Special needs adoption is supposed to work the following way: Children come into foster care on a temporary basis. Sometimes special needs babies are released at birth by their mothers, but are held in foster care until a family can be found. Other times a child is placed in foster care because of abuse or neglect by a parent. Still other parents can't cope with child-rearing for one reason or another and place their baby or child in foster care until they can. States are under a federal mandate, passed in 1980, to free a child for adoption if he cannot rejoin his family within a reasonable time.

Once free for adoption, the agency that is his legal guardian tries for a short while to place the child in an adoptive home within his county. If this is not successful, or if they believe he should be placed outside the county, the agency lists the child with the state adoption exchange. Other agencies with prospective parents they cannot serve contact these exchanges to get photos and descriptions of possible adoptees for their clients. Prospective adopters are also able to look through photo-listing books to find children to adopt.

If no home can be found for a child after being listed on the state exchange, he is listed on the regional exchange serving the surrounding states. Finally, he can be listed on a national exchange.

The system sounds efficient, but it doesn't work. It has been hard to find a fair balance between the rights of biological parents and the rights of children to live in a permanent home. Even children who are free for adoption can wait for years before they are listed on exchanges, and prospective adopters can find it hard to even get a home study.

These are the steps that should lead you through the system in the most efficient manner. Remember that practices differ in each state.

1. Call any parents group in your area and find out if they are active in special needs adoption (see page 47). If so, they can tell you which agencies might be most helpful. If you cannot find an appropriate group, call or write NACAC and they will tell you which group is closest to you.

2. Even though the parents group can tell you which agency will be most helpful, it is wise to call all the agencies in your area. As explained in chapter 5, you can get a list of agencies from your state adoption official and the Child Welfare League. Ask each agency what children they have waiting for adoptive homes. Tell them the kind of child you are looking for and ask if they have a guardianship (or custody) of any similar

children. Even if they say they have no such children, ask to be put on a waiting list, ask to come in and look at their state and regional exchange books, and ask about the possibility of a home study. Some agencies will do a home study and call other agencies and exchanges until they find a special needs child for you.

Keep accurate records of your calls, the name of the person with whom you speak and the replies you are given. These records will be valuable in selecting an agency if you get positive responses. If you get negative responses, you will want to check to see whether you were being given factual and appropriate information.

3. Your county department of welfare or social services should have a foster care and adoption division. They may be your best initial try, since they may know more about the foster care adoption situation in your area. They may have custody of more special needs children than any other agency. In addition, as a public agency, they will probably charge little or nothing for your home study.

   By law in some states you must be given a home study by your county agency if you are interested in a child on their state exchange book. This is because it is in the state's financial interest to lower the number of children in foster care. This does not mean that you are guaranteed pleasant or speedy service.

4. Some sectarian or private agencies willl give you a home study for a reduced rate if you are interested in adopting a special needs child—especially if you are interested in one of "their" children.

   Some agencies will give you a home study and then act as your representative. They will call exchanges and other agencies trying to find the kind of child you are looking for. These social workers often go out of their way to make personal contact with workers in other agencies and help find children that are not even listed on the exchanges.

5. There are some agencies that exist only to place special needs children. They work with children other agencies cannot serve. Like the exchanges, the children they list often have more severe problems, but this is not always the case. (See Appendix C for a list of these agencies.) Call them if you cannot get a local agency to help you.

6. Call your regional exchange headquarters if you have not been able to see photo-listing books of available children (see Appendix D). Your state might be one of the few without such a book, but every state is served by a regional exchange. Some states prohibit prospective adopters from seeing the books—they are for professionals only. Most states believe it is worth trading a child's right to privacy for the chance that an adopter will see his picture and become interested.

   It is in your best interest to see as many state and regional books as you can. Some states have less seriously handicapped children listed than others. Furthermore, looking at these books can help you define or broaden your concept of the kind of child you can accept. It is not unusual for a couple to want a baby initially and end up wanting a ten-year-old.

   Your regional exchange should be able to tell you where you can see the books. Often adoptive parents groups have the books or can get them for you.

7. By now you should have been able to get a home study. Your home study will be similar to what has been described earlier in the book. In addition, you will be asked questions about why you want a special needs child. Your social worker will be trying to see if you have a realistic view of what you are getting yourself into. She will want to know if you have the patience and flexibility required to deal with a special needs child. Will you take it personally if the child acts disruptive or talks glowingly about a former parent? Will you have the strength to set firm limits on his behavior while being loving at the same time? Will you become overwhelmed by his handicaps or prob-

lems? Raising a special needs child is a difficult and often thankless task. The home study is designed to make sure you are prepared for it. The social worker is trying to spare you and the child from the heartbreak of an adoption that does not work.

On the other hand, there are some agency workers who do not believe that a special needs adoption is a positive choice. If your social worker is being unfairly negative about your requests, talk to her about it. If the situation is not resolved, discuss the situation with the director of the agency and request a new social worker.

The newest concept in home studies is the group home study. This involves meeting with other prospective parents and discussing the problems and pleasures of special needs adoptions. You will meet other parents who have adopted such children and get to hear firsthand about their lives. Finally, you will probably get to write up your own evaluation and final home study report. Social workers who espouse the group study method believe that prospective parents can make their own decisions about whether or not special needs adoption is for them after attending five to twelve of these meetings and having at least one individual consultation with a social worker. One worker says that in hundreds of such home studies, there has only been one couple who decided they wanted to adopt and she disagreed about their ability to parent.

8. After your home study, or sometimes before or during it, you may be told of a child that interests you or you may see such a child in the exchange books. Your social worker will request a picture and full description of the child, his background and his personality. In some agencies, videotapes of the child are available. If you are still interested, a meeting can be arranged.

   For a special needs baby adoption, follow the procedure that is listed in chapter 5. The following procedure is for a somewhat older child.

9. You can often arrange to see the child in a setting where he will not know he is being observed. You might look at him through a one-way mirror or in a restaurant sitting at a nearby table. If you get a good feeling about the child, a meeting can be arranged.

10. The first personal meeting will probably take place in a zoo or a playground where there are distractions to ease tensions. This will be an awkward situation for both you and the child. It is good to have something in the surroundings to talk about. You may not like the child, much less love him. But if in spite of these feelings you are drawn to him and have a desire to make a commitment to him, the plans will progress.

11. After that first meeting, the social worker will talk to you and the child separately. If both of you are willing, another meeting will be arranged.

12. The number of meetings depends on your feelings and the policies of the agency with legal guardianship of the child. If you are meeting a child in another state, you will probably have to travel there and stay a few days to get to know him. It would be too risky to have him come to your home sight unseen.

13. You may wish to have the child visit in your home before he comes to live there permanently. Finally, when you and the child decide the time is right, he will move in with you. A young child's consent may not be actively sought, but the older child is considered a partner in the adoption. Older child adoptions are more like marriages, where both parties agree of their own free will to try and make a life together.

14. The child will live in your home for at least six to twelve months before adoption is finalized. During this time, it may be in your best interest to have individual or family counseling to help an older child come to terms with his past and to fit himself into your family. Some of the agencies offer up to eighteen months of casework to families for this purpose.

What about costs? Travel costs to meet the child, especially to another state, are usually paid for by the adopters. If you decide to invite him to your home, he will probably be brought there at no cost to you.

There is often a subsidy for adoption costs. If your income is not high and you are adopting a child officially designated as having special needs, you may be eligible for a subsidy to pay for his living expenses. If your income is high, you may still be eligible for a subsidy to pay for any special medical or psychological treatment the child requires. Your adoptive parents group or agency should be able to give you information on the subsidies that almost every state offers.

Do not be embarrassed to ask about subsidies. Some adopters are afraid to ask for fear of appearing mercenary. Showing your care and concern by parenting does not mean that you have to impoverish yourself, too.

Do not expect your agency worker to mention the subsidy—often you must ask. Sometimes the worker will not be aware of subsidies. In rare cases, a worker might want to avoid it because of the paper work. Persist. If no subsidy is available, your parents group or NACAC may be able to help you find other local help. Often, for example, parents groups keep lists of lawyers who finalize special needs adoptions for minimal fees. They also may know of doctors and therapists who charge moderate fees or organizations who provide services for handicapped children.

What if you haven't been able to find a child who meets your needs? Or even an agency to help you? If you live in a rural county, there may be few children available for adoption locally. The rule of thumb is that the more urban areas in your county, the more children will be available. Urban problems tend to disrupt families, and thus more children become eligible for adoption. You may have contacted agencies supervising many children in foster care, but few free for adoption. Or "their" children may be free for adoption, but the agency is not releasing them because the children are in a good foster home or the children have not been properly prepared for a move. The agency should probably offer you a home study and put you on the waiting list until one of their children becomes available.

Anytime you feel like you are getting the runaround, go through the proper channels to find out what is wrong—be pleasant but persistent. The place to start is the agency director. Next, you may wish to speak to the state official in charge of adoption. Your state official should be interested in correcting any situation where children are being held for an overly long time in foster care, or where prospective parents for foster care children are not being served. Find out who licenses adoption agencies in your state. They should also be notified if an agency is not serving the children in care.

Your elected officials and federal officials also have an interest, since foster care is funded by tax dollars. The Adoption Assistance and Child Welfare Act of 1980 calls for a review of each child in foster care. After eighteen months in care, agencies are supposed to make definite plans to return the child to his home or free him for adoption. These regulations are designed to prevent children from becoming trapped in foster care for year after year, but there is no guarantee that the regulation will be properly funded, applied or enforced.

Not every applicant can or should adopt a special needs child. If your agency is rejecting your application, you should be told directly and given a reason. On the other hand, in many areas agencies are not being as responsive as they should be to special needs children. One study, for example, showed that only half of special needs applicants in New York City were even screened by agencies in 1979, while thousands of children were legally free and waiting for homes there.[11]

If you are looking for a relatively healthy child under six years old, foreign special needs adoption may be a good option. In some areas of Latin America, for example, dark-skinned Indian or part Negro babies are considered very hard to place. Children older than infancy or even with correctable medical problems often are destined to grow up in institutions. Read chapter 8 on international adoptions. There are millions of children worldwide who need a home.

Another option you may wish to consider is becoming a foster parent. Your county foster care department can give you information about this. Usually social workers have some idea about whether or not a child can be returned to his biological home when he enters foster care. Some children who will not return or who are being freed for adoption may be available for preadoptive foster placements. Agencies are usually happy to place a child with foster parents who might want to adopt him if he becomes free, since this means fewer disruptions for a child. Foster parents are almost always given the first opportunity to adopt a child in their care if he becomes free.

You will be paid to care for the child while he is in foster care, and you will get the chance to be of service to a child who is going through a very sad crisis in his life. Whether he is coming to you directly from his biological parents or after several foster placements, he will be a hurt and confused child. He may not be able to show it, but he will be in desperate need of a solid, secure home where people truly care about him.

You must be able to give your love freely, knowing that you are taking the risk that he may return to his biological family. In fact, you will have to be sure that you do not bind him to your family so strongly that a return would be disastrous for him. It takes a strong person to give love freely and abundantly to a child under those circumstances.

What can you expect once a special needs child joins your family? The odds are three to one in your favor that the adoption will be successful, but that does not mean that it will be love at first sight, or that adjustments will be easy.

If there are other children in the family, prepare them for what to expect. They should become comfortable with any disability your new child will have, or at least they should be free to discuss any negative feelings they have with you. Give the existing children responsibility for making the new one fit into the family and that should lessen sibling rivalry. You will tell all the children they are brothers and sisters now, but do not expect anyone to really feel it for a while. Love is something that grows.

If he is old enough to understand, many people suggest that you help your new child prepare a scrapbook—a place where he can keep any old photos or momentos from his past life. A place where he can record impressions of his new family and memories of his old one. It will be important to talk with him about his past, even if it was painful, so he can make peace with it . . . and you can, too. It is also possible to let your child see the file of letters and contacts you made to find him. Any child adopted is indeed a wanted child—you had to want him very much to go through the hassle of getting him. To a child who has probably felt unwanted most of his life, it may be very reassuring to see tangible proof of how much you wanted him. But do not do this trying to elicit gratitude.

Try to hug the child often and tell him you love him. It might seem awkward at first, but it will feel more and more natural. It will give you a sense of belonging to each other. Hug the other kids, too, if there are others, and expect a bit of jealousy. Sibling rivalry is normal, but can be kept under control by praising any evidence of family sharing.

At a very basic level, an older child who comes into your home will not believe you will keep him. No adult has before. He has had many promises broken. It might hurt too much to believe again, only to find it all taken away. He may be on his own best behavior for a while, give you a "honeymoon" period for fear you will send him back. When he gets comfortable he may really test you with bad behavior to see if you will continue to love him. Comfort the fear, but discipline behavior that hurts himself or others. He needs help to gain control of himself and to find positive ways of handling anxiety and relating to others.

Your testing period may begin right away, even without a honeymoon. One young adoptee socked his new grandmother in the eye on their first meeting. She let him know in no uncertain terms that just because she was part of his new family, she was not going to allow herself to be used as a punching bag. They established a truce and later became the best of friends. When the testing is over, everyone can settle down to being a family.

Any older child will probably be behind his years in emotional and social development, but he will usually catch up given time and love. On the other hand, he may act much older than his age if he has never had the chance to relax and be a carefree child. He may regress when he begins to trust you. Again, he will grow out of it with time and encouragement, when he is ready.

He may miss his foster parents and speak glowingly of them. Try to be glad for him if they were good people. Also, try to understand that if he speaks well of them or his biological parents, it is not a negative reflection on you—even if he says it is! He is merely trying to gain a sense of security, telling himself if you reject him, there is someplace in the world he can go, someone who will protect him. He will let go of it when he trusts you and develops more positive feelings of self-worth.

He may not make friends easily. Don't forget, friends were never a permanent part of his life before. He may have learned not to begin liking anyone too much, because it hurts too much to say good-bye to them.

He may tell you about his horrifying experiences. If so, he needs to talk about them, even if they are upsetting to both of you. It can grind a parent up inside to hear how someone deliberately burned or beat their defenseless child. Try and keep the conversation open as long as he wants to talk. If he stops, let him know he can talk to you about his past whenever he needs to. How to respond to upsetting tales? Reflect his feelings. For example, if he is telling you about past abuse, say something like, "That must have hurt so much." He will feel understood and know that he can continue if he wants. If instead you reply, "Your mother was really bad to do that," he may feel disloyal revealing more or maybe he will decide he is bad too, since he was part of her.

What about the initial adjustment period with a transracial or handicapped adoptee? In both cases, an adoptive parent may feel strange at first. Holding or bathing a child of a different race, you may notice the color of his skin or texture of his hair. This reaction lessens as the bonds between you strengthen. It is normal to respond initially to a person's appearance, but as you get to know them, you begin to "see" them more in terms of personality than looks.

There can be an initial shock or even revulsion when dealing closely with a medical problem or deformity, but those feelings lessen as you get to know the child. It is important to guard against continuing feelings of pity. The DeBolt family tries to raise their handicapped children to be competent, confident and capable—and they succeed by never allowing self-pity. One family rule is "You don't ask people to do things that you can do yourself." Watching a person struggling across a room on crutches trying to retrieve an object you could easily get up and hand to them can be very difficult. You can feel heartless. Praising the child for his efforts and helping him devise efficient ways around his handicaps are far more helpful in the long run than waiting on him. You can't protect him from the hurts and difficulties of life, but you can help to make him strong enough to survive them.

Even with these tips and guidelines, you must find your own way to handle situations. Feel free to call your social worker and ask for her assistance, stressing that you care for the child, but he stumps you sometimes. In many good agencies, your caseworker will be available for regular counseling for up to eighteen months, in recognition of the difficulties many families encounter trying to assimilate a special needs adoptee. Other agencies offer little in the way of support, although all agencies arranging special needs adoption should provide the backup necessary to minimize disruptions.

Many adoptive parents groups have lists of family counselors who can be called on if help is necessary. These counselors must have a positive view of adoption, especially special needs adoption, but they should also recognize that many of the older adoptees bring past scars with them that must be worked through.

One couple adopted a teen-ager who began to steal. They consulted a family counselor, one who had not been recommended by an adoptive parents group. During their first meeting he asked, "What problem in your marriage resulted in your inviting trouble into your home?" They left, found another more sensitive counselor, and today their son is an upstanding member of the home and the community.

Thousands of parents have adopted special needs children and found it the most satisfying and rewarding experience of their lives. If you think you are up to the challenge, and if you think you can, as one mother put it, "love a rose with thorns," then special needs adoption may be for you. It has special challenges and special rewards, and rarely a dull moment.

7

Independent Adoptions

Janice and Art always wanted children and mourned the many miscarriages that Janice had over the years. Finally, they decided it was too painful to continue trying to give birth when they could love an adopted baby. By the time they reached this decision, however, Art was over forty and thus past the acceptable age limit to adopt a baby through agencies. Through friends they heard of a lawyer in another state and adopted their son through him.

Bob and Karen always knew Bob could not father children. They planned instead to adopt and were shocked to find out the wait for a healthy baby at agencies in their area was about four years. Even though they were only in their twenties, they felt this wait was too long. They contacted an adoptive parents group that gave them the names of some reputable people arranging independent adoptions. Bob borrowed the money to pay the birth mother's medical expenses and other adoption fees, and although they will be in debt for several years, they feel their decision was worthwhile.

Ada and Lou live in a state where agency adoptions are usually required to be between birth parents and adoptive parents of the same religion. Ada and Lou are Jewish, but so few Jewish babies are placed for adoption that they could not even get on agency waiting lists. They placed an ad in several newspapers saying they would give a good adoptive home for any baby. A lawyer arranged the adoption of their daughter when a pregnant girl answered their ad.

Independent adoptions do not involve adoption agencies as go-betweens. Instead, a doctor, lawyer, clergyman or friend acts as intermediary between the biological mother and adoptive parents while keeping their names confidential. In another form of independent adoption, called "open adoption," the prospective parents and birth mother make the arrangements directly, with no attempt to hide their identity. Some states do not allow independent adoptions and some only allow open adoptions.

Why would someone choose to adopt privately? In some states, most agencies have closed waiting lists, so prospective parents who want a healthy American baby have no alternative but independent adoption. In other cases, people who would make excellent parents may not be accepted by agencies because they are unable to meet questionable agency criteria regarding religious affiliation or age.

Then there are those who believe that adopters should have the right to avoid disclosing and discussing all the intimate information requested by agencies. Most reputable go-betweens will ask prospective adopters about the same personal matters as agencies, but their questioning will be less intense and less lengthy.

Birth mothers choose private adoption for several reasons. Many need to have their medical and/or living expenses paid during pregnancy. Most agencies do not provide full payment for medical expenses and often only can suggest welfare as a means of support. Some birth mothers want to select parents for their child, to directly place their baby with adopters or work with a go-between who will allow them to select between the biographies of several clients.

Finally, some birth mothers want to avoid agencies because they do not want to participate in the intense counseling agencies give. Friends and family often subject unwed mothers to a great deal of criticism for giving up "flesh and blood," so many birth mothers would rather work through a doctor or lawyer who readily accepts their decision to choose adoption.

Couples who investigate independent adoption may also find themselves criticized, because while such adoptions are legal in most states, black market scandals have given them a bad name. A black-market adoption involves an illegal or shady practice. The most common black-market offense involves fees so high that it appears either the birth mother or the go-between is selling the baby for profit, which is illegal. Black marketeers may pressure an unwed mother into surrendering her child, or may hire a woman, sometimes a prostitute, to get pregnant and sell the baby. They may not use accurate or legally correct forms and records.

Any of these illegal practices can make the ensuing adoption invalid. While the laws against black-market adoptions are often not enforced, you do not want to take this chance, or open the possibility that the birth mother may be able to revoke her surrender because of an invalid release. In fact, there have been cases where black marketeers have sent blackmailers to the adoptive home threatening to invalidate the adoption or reclaim the baby.[1]

Adoptive parents are frequently denied the right to have legitimate background information on their child, or to have a pediatrician of their choice examine the baby before they take custody. Parents have been given babies with serious handicaps and they have little recourse in a black-market adoption.

The black market in babies does exist, and it gives independent adoption a bad name. However, there are many highly reputable lawyers and go-betweens who arrange legitimate private adoptions. Furthermore, a recent study showed that in general there is no difference between the birth mothers who choose independent over agency adoption; they often merely need more financial support than the agencies can provide.[2] The same study showed that the predominant difference between adoptive parents who choose private adoption over agencies is that, as a group, they are better educated and of a higher socioeconomic status.

It is easy to recognize a classically bad black-market deal where a shady character exchanges a baby of unknown origin for a large sum of money in a parking lot. In most cases, however, the line between a black-market and a legal exchange is fuzzy. However, there are some important precautions that you can take to protect yourself.

1. Find out the laws governing independent adoption in your state. Call the state official who oversees adoption and find out whether independent adoptions are legal (see Appendix A). Some states will not permit them. Other states will not allow a go-between to arrange them or allow any advertising for a baby. Find out what laws govern independent adoptions, including what sort of release must be obtained from the birth mother and father. If you are considering an out-of-state adoption, what are the laws governing such adoptions in your state and the state where the baby resides? Some state adoption specialists may have a bias against independent adoptions. They may not be pleasant about giving you the information, but this is part of their job. Some adoption experts suggest that you hire a lawyer other than your go-between to advise you about the legality of any adoption agreement.

2. Select an absolutely reputable go-between. Your go-between must be someone you can trust and his reputation should be impeccable. Furthermore, he should be effective; some lawyers will charge large fees to "look" for a baby even though they rarely find them.

   It is safest when you have been referred to the go-between by an adoptive parents group, someone you know who will disclose the details of their adoption to you or a gynecologist or lawyer you trust. If this is not the case, will the go-between give you one or two references to check? Have there ever been any scandals associated with this person? Is this person a known and respected member of the community and/or of his profession? How many adoptions has he arranged? Does he have a specific birth mother in mind for you? If not, approximately how long does he estimate the wait will be? How does the go-between find birth mothers? How many babies does he work with each year?

3. Pay only reasonable and itemized fees. In a typical independent adoption where a lawyer is the go-between, it is customary for the adoptive parents to pay for his fee, doctor and hospital expenses of the birth mother

and baby, any travel expenses of any party involved, the legal fees of any out-of-state lawyer and possibly some of the living expenses of the birth mother during pregnancy.

You should be given an itemized breakdown of the costs of each of these items so that you know how much is going to lawyers, doctors and the birth mother. Are all these fees reasonable or are they so high as to make it appear that the baby is being sold for profit?

You can check the typical obstetric costs and the average hourly or flat rates lawyers charge in your area. One respected lawyer estimates that in 1980 a reasonable legal fee could range from $500 to $2,500. He says that anytime the total costs of an independent adoption runs $10,000 or more, he would assume it is a black-market deal.

Similarly, it is frequently legal to pay the living expenses of the birth mother during pregnancy, but these costs should be reasonable. Paying for an elegant vacation or for future college expenses may be construed as a sale.

It is not uncommon for a lawyer to charge a small fee, up front, that is not refundable even if no adoption occurs. Also, it is not unusual for the prospective adoptive parents to have to pay the medical expenses even if the baby is born dead or they reject it for some reason. However, the prospective parents should not have to assume responsibility for the child if it is born with a handicap.

Once a birth mother has been selected for you, you will probably be asked to put a sum of money in escrow toward her medical expenses. It is impossible to predict in advance exactly how much the medical expenses will be, since they may vary with complications.

4. Have as much or as little contact with the birth parents as you desire or as is legal. Couples can arrange an open adoption directly with the birth mother. In some states, the birth mother must place her baby directly with adopters, not using a go-between to hide identities. There have even been some successful cases where

the adopters agreed to let the birth mother keep some contact with the child.[3] Both parties were comfortable with the arrangement, but most adopters would not be.

In fact, many couples shun open adoption for fear that the birth mother may try to keep contact with the child. Since birth parents surrender all rights to the child in adoption, the adoptive parents can probably legally bar any visits to their child while he is a minor, but many parents do not want to even risk that the birth mother might show up. They want their names kept utterly confidential.

In some states, the birth mother must sign papers giving custody directly to the adoptive parents and, thus, will see their names on the consent papers. It is not uncommon for lawyers to present birth mothers with blank papers to sign, but in some states this is not legal. In other states, the birth mother can turn temporary custody over to the go-between so that complete confidentiality can be maintained for all.

Some lawyers recommend that a confidential (no names) meeting be held between the birth parents and adoptive parents. In this way the adoptive parents can have any questions answered about heredity, and do not have to have lingering or upsetting unanswered questions. Such a meeting is also beneficial to the birth mother, since she can get a comfortable feeling about her child's future and know he will grow up in a loving home. This is the prime concern of most birth mothers.

Some experts believe that if there were more of these meetings there would be fewer searchers or later meetings between adopted children and birth parents, because the birth mothers would get a better sense of resolution about their decision, and the prospective parents would get more of the information needed to answer their child's questions in the future.

Adoptive parents who do not want any direct meetings with the birth mother should be able to get a complete medical and sociological history of the birth parents and relations. They should be free to ask any question about the birth parents, except for their names and addresses, and be given a straight answer.

5. Get the information you need about the baby before you take custody. Some prospective parents are not concerned about the physical condition of the child. They believe that they are taking the same risks as they would take if they were having a biological baby. The important point is that you should have the right to have a pediatrician of your choice examine the baby *before* you take custody. If you are adopting an out-of-state baby, the head of obstetrics at the hospital in which your baby is born can recommend a pediatrician to examine the baby in the hospital, or the county medical society can recommend an independent pediatrician. Whether or not you care about whether the baby is "perfect," it is a good precaution to have the baby examined to determine his physical condition.

   You should also get information about the baby's birth and delivery. Was it an easy or hard birth? What was his weight at birth? Any complications? Was anesthesia used? This information could help diagnose any problems that develop at a later date.

   As previously discussed, many experts believe that your child will be more secure if you get as much information about his biological background as possible so that you can answer any questions he raises as he grows. It is also extremely important that you find out why his biological parents are placing him for adoption. Adoptees can understand if they know the reason, whether it be because of illegitimacy or other reasons. It gives them the sense that their biological parents made a positive plan for them by choosing adoption, instead of taking it as a rejection from birth.

6. Check to be sure the consent or release is valid. Check with state authorities and double-check with a lawyer to determine what sort of consent is legal. It varies by state. Some states require a waiting time between birth and release. This is often wise anyway, so the mother cannot claim she was under sedation when she signed.

What sort of forms must legally be used? Must a representative of the state social service department oversee the transaction to make it legal? How does it have to be written? Where does it have to be filed?

Did the birth father give his consent? If the birth father is known, he must sign a consent to have a valid adoption. If his whereabouts are unknown, you must advertise for him. In many instances, the advertisements are placed in obscure legal journals, but the letter of the law must be met if you are going to be protected. Similarly, if a birth mother is legally married, but the birth father is another man, in some states both men must sign the consent for the adoption to be legal.

Now that you know the basics of how to protect yourself against a black-market adoption, the larger and more difficult issue is left—how do you find your baby?

The first step is to tell everyone you know that you are interested in an independent adoption, and to ask if they know anyone who can give you information or help. It is amazing how large a list can be compiled this way. Friends have friends who have adopted privately, and many, especially those who have not engaged in black-market deals, are willing to share the names of those who helped. Other friends may be able to lead you to an unwed pregnant girl.

A word-of-mouth campaign is often very effective, but you must be very comfortable with the concept of adoption before you begin. This comfort is necessary to develop, as discussed in Part I, for a successful adoption anyway. Anyone who cannot spread the word among their friends that they are interested in adoption, may not, in fact, be ready for adoption.

Before you begin a word-of-mouth campaign, you must determine how comfortable you are dealing directly or even in a thinly disguised manner with the birth mother. If you did hear of a pregnant girl, how would you handle the arrangements? Do you need a lawyer or trusted friend to act as a go-between?

At the same time you are asking friends (and anyone else you meet), ask your gynecologist or any other gynecologist you know. Do they know of a pregnant woman who might be interested in adoption? What lawyers would they refer an unwed mother to for an independent adoption? If they have never done this, what colleagues can they name who might have made such a referral? Do they know any gynecologists on army bases or college campuses who might know of unwed mothers in no position to raise their babies? Can you find the names or get a personal referral to talk to anyone at an abortion clinic who can tell you what lawyer they refer women to who change their minds or whose pregnancies are too advanced to terminate? Can you get a similar referral to someone at a right-to-life or planned parenthood counseling center? Or are you comfortable calling such places and just trusting to fate that counselors will share such information with you? Keep a list of every name you get. Call each one and tell them of your desire to adopt.

Ask similar questions of your clergyman and lawyer, or any clergyman or lawyer you meet. The yellow pages of your local phone book may list lawyers under specialties like adoption; call and find out if they assist couples to find babies, and if they do, how many adoptions have they assisted in recently? If you run into dead ends, see if your librarian can help you look up articles that have been written about adoption that might quote local lawyers who specialize in that field.

Is it legal to advertise in your state to find a pregnant woman looking for a good, loving adoptive home for her baby? If so, are you comfortable placing such an ad using your telephone number or using a trusted go-between? Some couples have separate telephone lines installed with an unlisted number to use in advertisements and to protect their confidentiality. Ads can also be placed in newspapers in areas of the country where you hear babies are "more plentiful." This is frequently the case in Sun Belt states, but check to see if such advertisements are legal. Say you will accept collect calls.

A good source of information is often adoptive parents groups in your state. These groups are made up of active, dedicated volunteers who have been through the pain, frustration and ultimate pleasure of adoption. They are often willing and able to help with accurate information about go-betweens.

By calling or writing these groups you may get invaluable referrals to go-betweens or tips about successful methods to find babies in your state. If, at this time, there seem to be no babies available in your state, do not despair. Try calling adoptive parents, clergymen, doctors or lawyers you know, or adoptive parents groups in Sun Belt states. These states frequently have a large number of unwed mothers who have gone there "for their health," that is, to have their babies in a pleasant climate without anyone at home knowing about it. Not every state allows nonresidents to adopt independently.

Before contacting adoptive parents groups, keep in mind that these are volunteers, people who operate out of their kitchens with no expense budget except their own generosity. Do not call and ask them to return your call, especially if it is long distance. Do not write without enclosing a stamped, self-addressed envelope. And if they are helpful, seriously consider making a donation to their group.

Be aware that some adoptive parents groups do not approve of independent adoptions, and others are particularly dedicated to serving the needs of special needs children or foreign children. If you speak to someone who puts you down for wanting a white healthy baby, do not be discouraged. You will eventually find someone to help and understand your needs.

If this chapter makes independent adoption sound like a disorganized and serendipitous process, that's because it is. There are no nationwide practices, policies or conditions. The situation or prejudices that exist in one county or state may be completely different in another.

For example, in researching this chapter, I called a county bar association referral service and asked for the name of a lawyer who could assist in an independent adoption. Independent adoptions are perfectly legal in this county, and I made it clear I was interested only in a completely legitimate adoption. However, the head of the referral service berated me for fostering the black market. When I called another county referral service, they were gracious and helpful.

Unfortunately, you may encounter many dead ends. You may encounter many rude, harried, unhelpful people, but you will also encounter some very kind and caring people. Tenacity is the name of the game.

Once you have the names of several lawyers or go-betweens who can possibly help you, write or call them. Tell them a little bit about yourself and your spouse. Let them know why you want to adopt, why you think you would make good parents and what kind of child you are looking for. Find out about the fees they charge, how promising they can be about finding you a baby and how reputable they seem by asking the questions found at the beginning of this chapter.

After you have found your baby, the only thing left is to make him legally yours. Chapter 9 describes the procedure. He will then officially be your legal and legitimate child and heir—yours to love for the rest of your life.

8

International Adoptions

After the painful discovery that they could not have children, Martha and Bill decided to adopt a baby from Korea. They had always had positive feelings about Asian people and cultures and knew they could love a Korean child. They worked through an American agency with direct ties to a Korean orphanage. One of the happiest days of their lives was when they drove to the airport to meet their son.

Janet and Fred wanted a baby, but local and international agencies were not encouraging. They contacted a parents group that specializes in referring adopters to Latin American sources. A group member helped them select and contact an agency in Colombia. Within a year of application, they were notified that a baby was waiting for them. They flew to Colombia and brought the baby home themselves after a few weeks of processing the necessary adoption papers.

There are millions of abandoned or orphaned babies and children around the world in need of loving parents. Hundreds of reputable sources in many countries can help you adopt your child. In the last ten years, more than 30,000 foreign-born children were adopted by Americans, and the number grows rapidly.[1] More than 8,000 such adoptions will probably take place this year.

In Europe, the adoption situation is much like that in the United States. There is a "shortage" of healthy babies, but many special needs children are in institutions and foster care. Adoptable infants in Europe are usually only available to Americans with ancestral ties to the child's country. Most foreign adoptees come from developing countries.

If you are of non-Anglo-Saxon heritage, you may be able to adopt a child that fits "visually" into your family. Otherwise, by chance or by choice, you may adopt a child of an entirely different race. You must be able to see that child as your son or daughter, while recognizing the child's difference in a positive way. One mother lovingly described her child as a "beautiful brown berry." She would easily dismiss anyone who did not agree his brown skin was beautiful.

Like her, those considering international adoption should be somewhat color-blind. If you adopt a Caucasian baby, the child will probably be of Spanish extraction or from India, and will have darker skin than most Americans. In Latin America, there are a few adoptable all-Spanish infants, but most orphanages and agencies would be offended if you directly requested such a child. Your Latin American adoptee may be part or full Indian. Other international adoptees are of Negro, Malaysian, Oriental or mixed heritage.

Don't be reluctant to look at your deepest feelings about race. You will have to see your child as beautiful and special, and give him a good feeling about his heritage.

Successful international adopters feel enriched by cultural diversity and accept that their family will be interracial for generations. Unfortunately, this can mean that everyone in the family may be subjected to some discrimination and some unpleasant incidents throughout life.

Your best initial step when exploring foreign adoption is to contact adoptive parents support groups in your area that specialize in international adoption. You can find these groups through the *National Directory of Intercountry Adoption Service Resources* (see p. 87) or by calling your state adoption official (see Appendix A), or by contacting NACAC (p. 28).

Many of these groups hold meetings where their children attend so that prospective adopters can get a firsthand feel for foreign adoption and international families. Other groups that do not hold such meetings will introduce you to families who have adopted a foreign child. See if you can identify with these families. See what your response is to their children.

If there is no group near you, it would probably be worth a trip to attend a meeting of the closest group. Also, some groups are large enough to publish newsletters or information packets on foreign child-placing sources. While there is usually a modest membership charge, the services adoptive parents groups provide are invaluable and often free.

Examples of the larger groups that offer assistance are the Latin America Parents Association (LAPA) and OURS. LAPA publishes a newsletter and holds meetings for the public. They also offer specific, current information on many adoption sources and adoption procedures in Latin America. LAPA has guided many parents through a Latin American adoption and their help is free. If there is no LAPA chapter near you, then the national office (P.O. Box 72, Seaford, NY 11783) will help families in any state.

OURS is the largest adoptive parents group with over forty chapters. Their magazine can give you a good feel for life as an international family. They also offer information on child-placing resources as well as support services to prospective adopters. Their national headquarters is located at: 20140 Pine Ridge Drive, Anoka, MN 55303.

There are over seventy adoptive parents groups that provide the kinds of support and help needed by prospective international adopters. When you contact any such group, however, you should know that few, if any, have comprehensive knowledge of all the various child-placing sources. That information is found in the books described later in this chapter. Also be aware that some groups have a bias toward certain methods of adoption or certain countries. In spite of these factors, the best place to start is with adoptive parents groups that have special interests in foreign adoption. Remember they are volunteers, so send self-addressed, stamped envelopes if you contact them by mail.

When you adopt internationally, there are many countries where you can find your child. The following list shows some of the countries where American adoption agencies or adoptive parents groups can help you find your child. Read the list and see which evoke positive feelings. You will want to give your child a good feeling about his native land.

Argentina	**Domican Republic**	**Hong Kong**	**Peru**
Bangladesh	**Equador**	**India**	**Philippines**
Barbados	**El Salvador**	**Jamaica**	**Poland**
Bolivia	**Greece**	**Japan**	**Surinam**
Brazil	**Guatemala**	**Korea**	**Taiwan**
Chile	**Guyana**	**Mexico**	**Thailand**
Colombia	**Haiti**	**Nicaragua**	**Trinidad**
Costa Rica	**Honduras**	**Panama**	**Uruguay**
		Paraguay	**Venezuela**

When you adopt internationally, you also have a choice of three types of adoption methods. You can choose to adopt through an American-based agency, to adopt directly from a foreign-based child care source or to adopt independently through a lawyer or go-between. The methods vary in terms of how much initiative and responsibility you are expected to take in finding your child and bringing him to the U.S.

Agency Adoption: Adopting Through an Agency in the United States

Many states have an adoption agency that has direct ties to child-placing sources in one or more foreign countries. There are also some agencies in the United States that work with prospective adopters from other states, but their waiting lists may be longer than your local agency's. (See Appendix E.)

Some people prefer to work through an agency because they offer extensive pre- and post-adoption counseling. These adopters want to talk about international adoption with trained agency personnel. They also want the security of an agency; the knowledge that if something goes wrong before the adoption is final, the agency will usually assume responsibility for the child. Agencies guide adopters through the international requirements and usually arrange for the child to be brought to this country, instead of having the parents go to the child's country to bring him home.

On the other hand, many agencies have long waiting lists or restrictions as to the age, marital status and number of biological children their applicants can have. Many adopters want the freedom and flexibility other forms of international adoption offer.

Direct Adoption: Adoption Where the Parent Applies Directly to an Orphanage or Adoption Agency in the Child's Country of Origin

Parents can select a child-placing source abroad and make direct application, instead of using an American agency as an intermediary. Parents arrange for their own home study and collect the information needed to meet immigration and state adoption requirements. Adoptive parents support groups that specialize in foreign adoptions can offer invaluable assistance and are usually free. Consultants and lawyers with training in international adoptions are also available. Although experienced guidance is necessary, parents who choose this method are basically in charge of their own adoption proceedings. Usually parents fly to the child's country, often adopting there, or sometimes they arrange for an escort to bring the child to the United States.

This method offers several benefits. Parents often feel more in control. Also, some adoption professionals believe that parents establish a bond with their child and his culture more quickly and easily when they have been actively involved in the adoption and when they have flown to the child's country to personally escort him home.

Direct adoption can be a complicated process. You must satisfy the adoption requirements of your state, the adoption requirements of your child's home country and the immigration requirements of the federal government. Complicated, yes. Impossible, no. Jean Nelson-Erichsen, who has helped many couples and singles adopt directly from foreign sources, says that anyone with average intelligence and an average income can do it.

Independent Adoptions: Adopting Through a Lawyer or Private Intermediary in the Child's Country of Origin

Just as some people prefer to adopt independently through a lawyer or intermediary in the United States, some adopters prefer this method when adopting abroad. You may have more ability to control the color, sex and age of your child with this method. While it may be faster, there are risks. Your contact might not be scrupulous; this method might be expensive; and you will have to be extra cautious that you are observing the law of your state, the child's country and federal immigration. In addition, you will still need a home study and you may need a lawyer here and in your child's country, both of whom must be very familiar with adoption laws in both countries. In most independent adoptions, you fly to the child's country to pick him up. In others, you sometimes can arrange for an escort.

If you have a strong feeling about the kind of adoption you prefer or the country you prefer to adopt from, your choices may be limited. In some countries it is easier to adopt or only possible to adopt by one of the methods.

You can get this sort of information, plus timely and comprehensive advice on specific adoption sources from the following books:

1. *Report on Foreign Adoption.* This booklet lists active and competent agencies, adoptive parents support groups and direct sources that are working to unite prospective American parents and homeless babies and children. Some sources are American-based, others are in the child's country. Each year a new booklet is published and nine updates are sent out during the year, listing the frequent changes that occur in application requirements and availability of children. The report lists the kinds of children available from each source, the cost, waiting time and whether or not there are any restrictions for applicants regarding age, religion or marital status. It provides the most comprehensive and timely information available.

   It is compiled by dedicated adoptive parents who work on a professional, but unpaid, basis. To order the *Report on Foreign Adoption* and subsequent updates, send $5 to:

   International Concerns Committee
     for Children (ICCC)
   Anna Marie Merrill
   911 Cypress Drive
   Boulder, CO 80303

ICCC may be able to tell you about any foreign children available for immediate adoption in the United States because their adoption plans were disrupted by family problems. They may also be able to help you locate a foreign child (often with special needs) of specific sex and race if you want to register with them. When requesting information about these services, send a self-addressed, stamped envelope.

2. *National Directory of Intercountry Adoption Service Resources.* This directory is a state-by-state listing of the adoption agencies and adoptive parents support groups that are particularly active in international adoptions. It lists the agencies that conduct foreign adoption home studies as well as state officials and agencies that can provide information about the laws governing international adoptions. Ask your state official for any additions to the list of agencies and parents groups in your state.

   The directory may be somewhat out of date by the time you order it, but it will still give useful information. Be sure to check the listings of nearby states, since many agencies serve across state lines, but are only listed in their home state in this directory.

   Send a request for the *National Directory of Intercountry Adoption Service Resources* HEW Publication No. (OHDS) 80-30252 and a check for $5 to:

   Superintendent of Documents
   Government Printing Office
   Washington, DC 20402

3. *Gamines: How to Adopt from Latin America.* This book outlines the requirements and procedures for adoption in many Latin American countries. It also presents helpful information about how to contact foreign agencies and advises adopters on the best way to handle problems they may encounter. It includes specific information on adoption sources in Latin America, plus advice to help families adjust to cross-cultural or interracial life. It is $12.95 and can be obtained

through bookstores (the publisher is Dillon Press) or directly from the authors:

Jean Nelson-Erichsen and Heino Erichsen
Los Niños International Adoption
Information Center
919 W. 28th Street
Minneapolis, MN 55408

The Erichsens are adoptive parents who earned master's degrees specializing in adoption. They run adoption workshops and, for a fee, will provide individualized consultations by telephone or by mail for prospective adopters with special requests or problems. Write them for a list of the current services they provide, sending a stamped, self-addressed envelope.

4. *How to Adopt from Africa, Asia, Europe and the Pacific Islands.* In general, the *Report on Foreign Adoptions* covers most of the same countries as this booklet and lists sources that have more established American affiliations. This booklet is only for the most adventurous adopters who want to travel to the child's country to adopt. It tells about adoption procedures in over thirty countries, but many of the sources listed are only suitable for adopters who speak a foreign language or can spend considerable time abroad. This booklet is for those who want to know that they have considered every possible adoption source.

   It is written by the Erichsens and is a supplement to *Gamines.* To order it, write the Erichsens at the address listed above.

With these books and an affiliation with an adoptive parents group, you will have the information and support necessary to pick a country, a method and a specific adoption source. Now you can begin to find your child.

Which adoption method initially appeals to you? If you decided to try adoption through a United States-based agency, contact all in your state first. If these have long waiting lists or do not work with the kinds of children you could call your own, contact the agencies listed in Appendix E, which work throughout the United States. If these agencies cannot help, do consider a direct adoption. Many people have done it and found the experience itself worthwhile and rewarding. There are dedicated parents groups to help you, and they can be every bit as supportive as an agency.

If you decided to try an independent adoption through a lawyer in your child's country, do reconsider working through an orphanage or agency. Some people choose this route thinking that they would not be accepted by an agency. In fact, many agencies and orphanages in foreign lands have much more flexible requirements for their applicants than American agencies. People who cannot meet age, religion or marital status requirements for babies in the United States are often welcomed by foreign sources. With luck and effort, you can often find a foreign agency with a waiting time of about a year.

Some people choose the independent route because they are afraid of medical problems with orphanage children, or because many orphanage infants have been abandoned with heritage unknown. Our Immigration and Naturalization Service (INS) has to check children for retardation and major medical problems before they are cleared for a visa to the United States. In addition, you can have a pediatrician of your choice check the child before you take custody. (The local United States embassy can recommend a pediatrician.) This does not guarantee a problem-free baby, of course, but in life there are few guarantees, whether the child is biological or adopted.

If the prospect of adopting an orphanage child still frightens you, or if you can only accept a light-skinned Caucasian child, independent adoption may be for you. But consider whether your reservations indicate that international adoption is not really for you at all. If you want to proceed, read the previous chapter on independent adoptions to differentiate between legitimate and black-market adoptions.

You may be able to get the names of reputable lawyers who arrange adoptions by asking for such help from United States embassies in Latin America, or by contacting Latin American consulates in Washington. If you have any friends in international business, they may be able to help you find independent contacts. Some American adoption lawyers have international connections.

You will probably need the support and advice of an American lawyer familiar with adoption in your child's country and an adoptive parents group or someone like the Erichsens at Los Niños. Often adoptive parents groups are skeptical about independent adoptions, but they may help you anyway. The rules and regulations governing international adoption are tricky enough that you will need someone knowledgeable and experienced to advise you.

Have you decided to directly contact an agency or orphanage abroad? More and more adopters are using this method and finding it very rewarding. The following steps will give you an idea about the procedure. Before you read the list remember that although the procedure sounds complicated, many, many other people have done this and you can too. This list will give you an idea of the procedure and make you aware of some of the complications that can arise. Procedures and laws are different for each country, and they change all the time. Do not use these procedures without checking the current regulations with your state, the INS and your child's country.

1. Contact your state adoption authority to determine what laws and procedures must be followed for foreign adoptions. Ask whether your home study must be done by an agency, or whether it can be done by a licensed independent social worker. Also ask if they have an updated list of agencies and adoptive parents groups working with foreign adoptions.

2. Contact all the adoptive parents groups in your area and see which countries and adoption methods they are familiar with. They may be able to refer you to specific sources or to another group like OURS or LAPA that has special knowledge of foreign adoption. Affiliate with one of these groups. They will offer support and guidance before, during and after adoption. Plus, your child will have the reassuring experience of knowing other transcultural families.

3. Select one to four foreign adoption sources from the books listed above or from your parents group recom-

mendations. Write a letter introducing yourself, requesting an application and asking about the waiting period for the kind of child you want. Describe yourself and your family. If you want a child who looks as much like your family as possible, describe yourselves and ask for a child with similar characteristics. Send a picture if you like. Any more direct reference to race may be offensive to the person reading your letter, and this may hurt your chances.

Include information about your work, your home, the reasons why you want to adopt and why you would make a good parent. You can send the letter in English, or better, have it translated. If you are divorced, or are single, ask whether or not this will affect your application.

Send your letter air mail. Enclose enough international postage coupons (available from your post office) for a return reply. If you have not heard from the source in four to six weeks, write again.

Select from the replies the source that best meets your needs and make a formal application. Notify the other sources and thank them for their help. You may even want to send a small donation.

4. As soon as you send your inquiries abroad, contact your local Immigration and Naturalization Service (INS) requesting all necessary forms and instructions for an international adoption. Forms will include:

   I-600: Petition to classify an orphan as an immediate relative
   A-134: Affidavit of support
   FD-258: Fingerprint cards (two per spouse)

   Some INS offices require you to request these forms by phone or in person rather than by mail.

5. When you send your inquiry letters abroad, also begin checking home study sources. They vary in the time they take to begin and complete the home study, and in the amount they charge for the service. Adoptive parents groups can recommend home study

sources. Be sure the person who writes your study has experience dealing with the country of your choice.

6. Collect the information needed by the orphanage or agency you choose. Often these documents will have to be translated, notarized, verified and authenticated by your child's country's consulate in the United States. There are intricacies that you should know about, which, if not observed, can cause red-tape delays. Your parents group can advise you. For example, documents may have to be notarized by a notary who is registered in the county where the documents were obtained. Another example—birth certificates must be originals, with a raised seal. Typical documents required are:

   - home study
   - letters of recommendation from friends, clergy or employer
   - financial statements including a letter from employer, W-2 forms and IRS returns
   - medical reports on both adopters from a physician

7. Begin collecting the forms and documents you will need to send to the INS before you are assigned a child and request that they begin processing the forms as you intend to adopt "in the immediate future." The documents for the INS will include:

   - a brief letter mentioning the country from which you will adopt
   - your completed I-600 and the $35 processing fee
   - completed fingerprint forms (The INS or your local police will fingerprint you. This form is then sent to Washington for approval. It can take eight weeks to process.)
   - birth certificate or proof of citizenship for each adopter
   - marriage license and/or proof of termination of prior marriage, if applicable
   - letter from your employer or accountant stating your position and salary

- financial statement from bank regarding your assets
- a copy of the home study

It is wise to take these forms and documents to the INS district office in person. The INS papers are valid for one year after they are filed. At the end of a year, most of your file will be destroyed *if* you do not notify them that you want to keep it active and update the necessary papers.

8. Make sure you have a valid passport in case you have to fly to your child's country and bring him home.

9. Be prepared for a wait. The wait can be from three months to two years depending on the source and method you choose. Regardless of how long it actually is, it can seem like forever.

One day you will be notified, by mail or by a collect call, that there is a child for you! You will probably be told something about the child and will be sent a picture and description. You can decide to accept this child or you can state valid objections and usually be given one more opportunity to adopt.

10. You will be sent the child's birth certificate, a certificate of abandonment, or release from the birth mother, plus a release from the agency or orphanage. Take these to the INS so that they can complete the work necessary for the visa.

11. You may have to take all the documents to your state court and get a preadoptive certificate for the INS.

12. The INS will complete its work and send the information to the consular office in your child's country so that they can issue a visa. They will issue an IR-3 visa if you are going abroad to adopt or an IR-4 visa if you intend to adopt here.

13. You will either fly to pick up your child or have him escorted to the United States. Many experts advise you to fly to his country if possible so that you can meet him and get to know his culture immediately.

14. Once home, you must register your child as an alien with the INS.

15. Follow adoption proceedings for your state to make him legally yours.

16. After adoption, apply for a valid birth certificate from your state. Your child will need this in future years as proof of identity. (Not all states issue these.)

17. After adoption, petition for citizenship. He will not automatically become a citizen on adoption. You must file an application for naturalization on behalf of a child. This form is available from the U.S. Department of Justice, Immigration and Naturalization Service.

18. Relax and enjoy your child! He is yours to love for life.

There have been few good studies on the success of foreign adoptions, but the opinion of those involved in such adoptions is overwhelmingly positive. As Elsa Eisenberg, one of the founders of LAPA says, "There are very few disruptions. (Cases where the parents do not finalize the adoption or the adoption falls apart.) I know of only one in the hundreds I've seen. There seems to be a minimum of problems."

What happens if there is a problem? Perhaps an older child is adopted and does not fit into the family. Perhaps a serious medical problem develops and the parents do not want the responsibility? These fears can be in the minds of many people considering international adoption, and they are certainly in the minds of government officials skeptical of foreign adoptions.

The answer is unclear. According to the *Intercountry Adoption Guidelines* developed by the Department of Health and Human Services, the placing agent (the orphanage or agency or intermediary) should be responsible for "the removal and replacement" of the child. There is a serious question about whether that would occur once the child is in the United

States. In the end, if neither the agency nor the family will take responsibility for the child, the state "should" assume the responsibility for finding a home for the child, according to the *Intercountry Adoption Guidelines*. In fact, this has occasionally happened. Adoptive parents groups, however, are usually able to find another home for the child without state help, and the ICCC—the people who publish the *Report on Foreign Adoption* (see p. 86)—have a clearinghouse to help with any disruptions.

What about special needs foreign adoptions? In some developing countries, minor handicaps like a cleft palate can make a child virtually unadoptable. Children older than infancy have a hard time being placed. Therefore, if you are interested in adopting a child who otherwise would not have a home, and if special needs children available in your locality would not fit into your family, consider this option.

The ICCC is also establishing a registry that will try to match families (or singles) and special needs foreign children with more serious handicaps. They will send pictures and descriptions of children if you register with them by writing to: 911 Cypress Drive, Boulder, CO 80303.

Foreign adoption sounds complicated, but taken step by step, it won't be overwhelming. Most people encounter very helpful and caring professionals once they make connections with foreign agencies and orphanages. There can be time delays and there can be government officials, both American and international, who seem to be opposed to your loving intentions. Why are some people thwarting, not helping, the cause of international adoptions?

Answers to this question can be found in position papers prepared for the International Year of the Child Secretariat at the United Nations.[2] Instead of promoting intercountry adoption, these papers stressed the need for adopting countries to help developing countries eliminate the need for international adoptions. Some countries view adoption as an act of aggression because blood and cultural ties are severed when these infants are taken from their country of origin. The papers cite the level of prejudice in Western culture and question whether adopted children will be exposed to discrimination. They also point to the number of waiting children in the United States and the fact that one third of the children in foster care in the

United States were placed for "temporary care" but have stayed for five to ten years. The papers call on adopting countries like the United States to address the problems of their own waiting children and to help developing countries eliminate the need for intercountry adoption. Regardless of arguments against international adoptions, there is the reality of millions of babies and children abroad who are in desperate need of homes.

There are children who need your love every bit as much as you need to give it, and international adoption can be a very positive experience for you and your child.

9

Waiting for Your Child

If your agency has completed a home study and approved you for one of "their" children or if your application has been accepted by a reputable foreign child-placing source or if an honorable attorney has accepted your retainer and assured you of a baby, eventually you will get your child. The big question is how long you have to wait.

Some sources can give you a relatively accurate estimate. They have a waiting list and can tell you about how long it will be until your turn comes. Other sources try to match the backgrounds of children and parents, or allow birth mothers to select parents from those waiting on the list, so it is harder to predict how long it will be before you are "matched" or a birth mother requests someone like you to parent her child.

It might seem that the difficult part of adoption is over now that you have been promised a child, but many adopters consider the wait the hardest part of all. Other adoptive parents can be very supportive during this time. They know what it is like to ache to hold a child of their own. They know how hard it is to believe that ache will ever go away.

Some people go through this waiting period without a doubt about what they are doing. One insightful adopter said, "While I was pregnant with my first child, I felt great ambivalence about whether or not I wanted a child. But during the time we were trying to adopt our second child, I felt no conflict whatsoever." Others are filled with secret apprehension. They know they are taking on a big responsibility and they get the jitters.

It is normal to wonder whether or not adoption is for you. Some people can only admit these doubts after their home study is approved. Most feel more comfortable discussing their fears with their spouse or other adoptive parents than with their social worker. This is the time to learn how to share your deepest concerns with your spouse; get in practice for the concerns that parenting will stir up through life.

There are several other constructive steps you can take during your wait. Get to know families with children like the one you plan to adopt. Observe the way they discipline and influence their children. Discuss this with your spouse and see if you agree on child-rearing practices. It is better to resolve differences and plan ahead than to find yourselves fighting over your child.

Many people waiting for a baby find it is painful to be around other people with infants. Seeing other families creates a longing that feels like physical pain. Try to familiarize yourself with children anyway, knowing that you will have a baby soon yourself.

If you are waiting for a child from another country, become familiar with his cultural heritage. Get to know people from his country; learn to cook some of their native recipes. If your child is older than infancy, he will speak a different language and will probably be bewildered by our customs. Remember, he has only been used to institutional living, which is pretty spartan in most countries. Talk to other parents who have adopted similar children. They can give you advice and teach you some phrases to speak to your child. You will not want to overwhelm your new child with toys or visitors at first, but he may be comforted by meeting another adoptee who speaks his language.

The plans you make for the arrival of an older American child will be similar. Your child will have been through many unhappy changes in his life and he will fear that your family will be no more permanent than his other ones were. It may take quite awhile for him to trust your love, and he will probably test it often.

Put yourself in his place and see what would make you

feel at home. One mother of a seven-year-old realized that when her four-year-old arrived, there were no toys in the house he could call his own. Everything had to be given or loaned by his new older brother. She thought that made him feel like a visitor, and indeed he did appreciate the few new things bought just for him. If your child gets to know other older adoptees, he may trust your good intentions sooner.

If your child will have other special needs, complete your research into all the support systems available. You may need to get your name on the waiting list for some of the services your child will need. Finding children with similar handicaps might help him feel more comfortable.

Look for a well-trained pediatrician with a positive view of adoption. Other adopters can give you a referral. Call and ask the pediatrician about his views of adoption. If he voices any doubts about inheriting problems, or makes any comments that seem negative, cross him off your list of prospective doctors. A change of water, diet or surroundings can make your new baby cranky or give him diarrhea the first few days. You will want a supportive doctor standing by. Similarly, you will want a doctor who can accurately diagnose any problems in an older child, and not just dismiss them or overemphasize past traumas.

Find out about adoption proceedings in your state. You can call the county attorney and find out what court has jurisdiction over adoptions. Investigate whether or not you have to formally change your will or medical insurance to include your new child. If you have not hired an attorney, decide whether or not you want one to represent you during your adoption hearings. If you adopt through a local agency, you probably will not need your own lawyer. If not, you may want to hire one. Compare fees of lawyers recommended by your parents group. In some states, like Maryland, it is reportedly fairly easy to file your own adoption and thus save the expense of legal fees.

Your state adoption official (see Appendix A) can give you information about adoption proceedings. In general, the procedure goes something like this:

1. You will file a legal document, a petition to adopt, requesting the court's permission to adopt. You will file

documents such as your birth certificate, your child's birth certificate, a report on your health and your child's health and a release from the birth parents.

2. During the time between the child coming to live with you and the final adoption, a social worker will visit to see that both you and the child are pleased with the arrangement. One study showed that social workers see themselves as helpful consultants during these visits, but adoptive parents are fearful of their criticism.[1] In fact, there is little to fear from these visits, since it is extremely rare for a child to be removed from the home unless the prospective adopters do not want to keep the child. It is very unusual for a social worker to recommend removing the child against the parents' will. To do so would require firm proof that the child's emotional or physical health was being threatened in a serious way by the adopters.

3. If you are waiting for a baby and worried that the birth mother might change her mind, check the laws. The release for adoption cannot be signed before the birth, but after it is signed the birth mother can not revoke her consent in most states, unless she can prove she was forced or duped into signing. If your state allows revocations for reasons other than duress, the birth mother rarely has more than thirty days after signing to change her mind (see Appendix B).

4. Your adoption hearing will probably take place about six months after your child comes to live with you. You can request a confidential hearing in the judge's chambers. It is usually a speedy and informal meeting held to determine that you want to make the adoption final.

5. When that final adoption order is signed by the judge, your child will finally, legally be part of your family forever.

6. You may have to request a new birth certificate for your child. This will list you as the parents and be useful for him when he needs identification in the future.

7. If your child is from another country, you will have to file a petition for naturalization on his behalf with the Immigration and Naturalization Service.

As the time approaches for your child to come to live with you, be sure to get a scrapbook and fresh film. You will want to record with pictures and words your feelings about his arrival. Looking at this book will become a favorite ritual in your house. It can also be a natural way to begin any discussions of adoption.

Part III

RAISING YOUR CHILD

10

What to Expect

First there is the question of how adoptive parents are to see themselves. Are they to regard themselves as just ordinary parents? Or are they to regard themselves as different?[1]

David Kirk
Sociologist and Adoption Researcher

In general, the problems that arise between parents and adopted children are the same as those that would arise given the same personalities and circumstances if the children were not adopted.[2]

Stella Chess
Child Psychiatrist and Researcher

Every new parent wonders what to expect from family life. The secret question many new adoptive parents have is, "Will it be the same as if I had a biological child?" Your child may grow up and wonder the same thing—"Would a blood tie make me feel differently?" Studies show that you will not feel differently nor will you have more problems just because you adopted, but some parenting tasks *are* different.

Unlike biological parents, you will have to tell your child

he was adopted and you will have to help him form a positive identity based on his dual heritage. You will have to be sure that the fact of adoption or the comments of others regarding adoption do not cause problems for your family. While you do have some additional tasks and concerns because of adoption, that does not mean you are going to have additional problems. In fact, if you handle those tasks well, they can add a positive dimension to family life. Talking about adoption can often force parents and children to communicate and to be sensitive and open to one another's concerns and feelings. Families formed by adoption can be under a special pressure to talk out their problems—and that can be very healthy.

This chapter will discuss what you can expect. It will try to explore some issues and areas that may be misunderstood by parents.

What to Expect at First

Parenting is one of life's most exciting, challenging, frustrating and rewarding adventures. Adoptive parents will experience the same roller coaster ride of emotions as any biological parent. Your child will probably elicit deeper feelings of love than you knew existed, but you will probably also learn the true meaning of frustration.

If you are going to be a successful parent, you must develop positive expectations. You must resolve at your deepest level to work through any problems that occur. Enjoy the positive feelings you have toward your child, but don't be afraid to acknowledge the negative ones. Only by knowing your own feelings will you be able to work through any problem.

Most parents have very idyllic expectations of seeing their child for the first time. Unfortunately, it is not always love at first sight, whether you give birth or adopt. Different people have different initial reactions to their children. Some feel an instant rush of love, but many have to fall in love slowly, over time. One father reluctantly admitted that while he liked his son from the beginning, he didn't feel a strong love bond for at least six months. One day he just woke up and knew that he would be devastated if the child was no longer part of his life.

One mother who had expected a Gerber baby, blurted out

"He's so ugly!" immediately after she gave birth. The nurses were shocked and let her know they thought she was deficient in maternal hormones. Actually, she was just as normal as the woman who is thrilled by the first sight of her baby. This woman, like most, soon began to see her child as beautiful, to develop that unrealistically distorted, but delightfully positive view that all good parents have of their children. Some people, however, never respond fully to infants; they find they prefer the companionship an older child can offer.

Initial reactions to a new older child can be equally unsettling. Some parents find themselves critically appraising the child like a newly acquired piece of furniture. Once the initial shyness and discomfort wears off, a more positive bond can form.

You may feel from the very first sight that your child is part of you. Or that feeling may have to grow. Regardless, sooner or later you will develop the deep conviction that this is truly your child—someone else merely happened to give birth. If you do not grow to feel this way, if secretly you do not feel like the real parent—a parent who has the right to both praise and discipline the child; a parent who feels spontaneous bursts of love for his child—you should probably get some counseling to help you overcome the issues that are keeping you from feeling your child is your own.

Having a baby or acquiring a child can cause drastic changes in life-style and self-image. You may adjust immediately without stress. Some people, however, who for years have thought of themselves as infertile, or who have grown used to the struggle of adopting, find it difficult to change their life-view when a child comes into their home.

If you adopted a baby, you may not have realized how very demanding that tiny person can be. At first, life can seem to be an endless round of bottles, diapers and comforting away tears. It's exhausting and some mothers who adopt experience the same postpartum depression as biological mothers, secretly wondering, "What did I get myself into?" If this happens to you, if you find yourself panicked that you have "done yourself in" by becoming a mother, try not to worry. The feeling almost always passes and love grows.

Don't react by becoming a guilty martyr. Be sure to take time for yourself and the activities you like. It is not healthy for you or your child if your life becomes completely child-centered. Be sure you also make time for you and your spouse to get away alone together. Every parent needs a little breathing space.

Richard Gardner in his book *Understanding Children* says it is psuedo-love when parents say, "He's everything I have in the world," or "I would never go to work and leave my child." Gardner says the healthy parent has sources of gratification other than his child. It puts too much pressure on a child to be the parents' sole focus. Gardner also frankly states that child-rearing is often boring and wearying work. Everybody needs a breather from it, and some need more than others.

Of course, if you find that any time spent with your child is tense and unsatisfying, get professional counseling to overcome the problem. The trick for most parents is to find their own unique, comfortable balance of time devoted to family and time devoted to individual pursuits. That way when you are with your child, you can give the time freely and happily.

You may be unprepared for the negative feelings that can occur if your baby cries for long periods of time. This is especially stressful when your sleep is repeatedly disturbed by inconsolable crying. New parents of older children may feel the same surprising anger if their child is very hyperactive or a consistent bed-wetter. The frustration, worry, tension, exhaustion and general feelings of helplessness can combine to make any parent fear they may become abusive. It is extremely important for husbands and wives to be mutually supportive of each other and to take over the child-care responsibilities until the person under stress, given a little rest, can regain his sense of empathy for the child. Single parents must find a relative or friend to help when necessary.

If you have adopted an older child, you can expect a "honeymoon" period when your child is on best behavior. Afterward, when he gets comfortable with you, there may be an opposite period of horrid behavior to test the strength of your commitment to him. He will be asking, "Do you love me enough to keep me even if I am bad?" You may ask the same question of yourself. Firmly tell him when you do not like his behavior, and use the discipline method that you are comfortable with, but at the same time, tell him he is your child forever.

Some international adoptees seem to have few adjustment problems. With others, the long plane ride, "foreign" American food and water, and incomprehensible hubbub on arrival may take its toll. The child may feel sick or cranky for a while. It may also be a strain if the child is old enough to have a language barrier. Love grows from your attempt to comfort and understand your child, especially if you do not get too worried about initial problems.

This section does not mean to imply that the first few weeks of family life will necessarily be difficult. Much depends on circumstances plus the temperaments of you and your child. Having a new child in the home is a big change, however, and change causes stress until the situation loses its strangeness. If you try to relax and not get upset about any initial adjustment problems, life tends to even out again.

As cited in the Introduction, studies show you should expect at least as much success and satisfaction as a biological parent feels. Whether you have adopted transracially or transculturally or not; adopted a baby or an older child; adopted a malnourished baby or a fat, healthy one; adopted the offspring of a criminal or college professor, studies show that the odds are heavily in your favor that your child will turn out to be healthy, well-adjusted and at least scholastically average.

Children tend to become more similar to their parents by adoption than to their biological relatives in terms of IQ, attitudes and moral codes. Your child may even come to resemble you as he picks up your habits and mannerisms. You will be the main influence on your child's life. You will be the real parent—even 87 percent of birth mothers in one study said that.[3]

On the other hand, fate may deal some unexpected problems to any parent—biological or adoptive. Children may not turn out to be healthy or loving. They may be slow learners, be unhealthy or have difficult temperaments. Those are the chances that each of us takes when we decide to parent.

There are certain things you can do to increase your chances of being a successful parent. Several studies[4] showed the importance of placing the family above all other concerns; the importance of giving the child a sense of being a valued and contributing part of a cohesive family unit.

The Key Factor of Temperament

Problems can occur if parents and children have different or conflicting temperaments. In the battle over nature vs. nurture, heredity vs. environment, some important research on temperament seems to get overlooked. Researchers into the subject of temperament[5] have concluded that many behavior problems and family problems can be related to unresolved clashes between the child's temperament and environment.

What is temperament? Researchers Thomas, Chess and Birch[6] studied children from infancy to adulthood and concluded that each child has his own temperamental style that can be detected in early infancy. It is a combination of nine different characteristics such as adaptability, amount of pleasant or unpleasant moods, attention span, activity level and responsiveness.

Most children have a pattern of those characteristics that makes them "easy children." They have regular eating and sleeping patterns, handle frustration rather well and adjust to new experiences without much upset. Unfortunately, the researchers found two other patterns that are more difficult to manage.

The "difficult child" is a rather negative child with irregular habits and intensely hostile reactions to new experiences. The first day of school or even a taste of new food or visit to a new place may evoke loud crying or tantrums. He is difficult to comfort or calm. This kind of child can make a parent feel angry or helpless.

"Difficult children" require a structured routine at home. New experiences have to be kept to a minimum. When a new experience is necessary, researchers suggest that parents firmly urge a child to try it six times. Tell the child that if he still hates it, he can give it up. Most difficult children accommodate themselves after the sixth try.

The other pattern that can cause trouble is the "slow-to-warm-up" child. This type of child is also negative to new experiences, but in a passive way. He may allow new food to stay in his mouth and then dribble out. He may cling to mommy when new people enter his world, and he may retreat to the sidelines in school rather than joining the group. Such a child can be exasperating, especially to a parent with a more active nature. In fact, such children will usually grow to enjoy activities if they are given time to adjust. Parents must be patient and willing to wait for a while while the child "warms up." Then they can gently encourage participation in the new experience.

Temperament seems to be inborn. Yet there is no evidence to suggest that parents of one temperament tend to produce children of the same temperament. There is no evidence that parents of children with difficult temperaments are any different from other parents. But they must use different techniques to cope with their child, otherwise life will be a constant, unpleasant battle. The important thing for adopters to remember is that if their child turns out to be difficult, or slow to warm up, or overly passive or active—blame it on temperament, not "bad blood."

The Adoption Paradox

Is adoption different or the same as biological parenting? Should parents and children try to ignore the fact of adoption or not? Louise Raymond, the respected adoption counselor and parent, gave the following paradoxical advice, "Always remember he's your own—and never forget he's adopted."[7]

Your child is your own. He is your real child and you are his real parent—expect both you and he to feel this. On the other hand, the fact of adoption must never be hidden. It is a fact of life. It may or may not affect your life, but it is a part of your child that must be acknowledged. If the fact of dual heritage brings dual assets—that's terrific. If the fact of adoption brings some insecurities—those are to be acknowledged and overcome.

The problems seem to come when families try to ignore the fact of adoption or, on the other hand, when they are all too sensitive about it.[8] Adoption should never be blamed for problems. Stella Chess, the child psychiatrist and researcher has written, "The types of behavior difficulties and parent-child conflicts are the same in adoptive situations and in situations where the parent-child bond is biological."[9] Unknown ancestry should never be made a scapegoat for problems by parents or by children. Some children do develop fears of unknown heritage or rejection because they are overly sensitive to adoption or misinterpret it. Parents must be alert to this. David Kirk, the sociologist and adoption researcher stated that the adoption paradox answer is "to acknowledge the difference."

Kirk quotes an adopted boy who said, "The child who is born into his family is like a board that's nailed down from the start. But the adopted child, him the parents have to nail down. Otherwise he's like a board in midair."[10] But don't many parents give birth to children who have to be "nailed down"? Aren't there many sensitive children or children who do not have easy temperaments, who have to be helped to feel secure in any family? These questions are part of the adoption paradox, too. Perhaps we are speaking of a larger paradox that affects all parents: Let them be themselves, but don't forget you have to guide them.

11

Telling Your Child About Adoption

Who is my real mother? he shouted.
I am, I said. I am your real mother by love and by law.[1]

Pearl Buck speaking to her child

How will I tell my child he's adopted? This question troubles most parents. Part of the confusion arises from the fact that "experts" have changed their opinion over the years about the best way to handle this aspect of adoption.

In the 1940s, agencies often advised telling the child his birth parents were dead. Others advised (and some still do) not telling at all; pretending he was not adopted. In the days when available children were so plentiful that adoption could be timed, some prospective mothers wore pillows under their clothes feigning pregnancy.

The trouble with "secret adoptions" is that the strain of keeping big family secrets can also strain communication and relationships. Plus, it is hard to keep adoption secret. Family and friends often let it slip, or the adoptee finds a document that reveals his adoption.

Thus, in the 1950s and 1960s agencies began to advise openness. Parents were encouraged to discuss adoption with their children, friends and neighbors. Some parents went overboard and would always introduce their child by saying, "This is my son. He's adopted." The theory was right, but the practice was forced.

Today a more relaxed openness is advised. Children need to know they are adopted and that adoption is a happy event. It should be an accepted and acknowledged aspect of life, but not dragged into introductions or conversations. Children tend to dislike anything that sets them apart from the crowd, so they may not want their adoption discussed in public or any fuss made about it. But they do not want their adoption kept secret.

Why is it so important to be relaxed and open about adoption? Studies have shown that most well-adjusted children know about their adoptive status from an early age.[2] They were told by their parents, not by an outside source, and they were free to discuss adoption and ask questions about it throughout their lives.

These studies also show that a high percentage of adoptees searching for birth parents were not told about adoption until late in life, or they were often told in a negative or angry manner, and were not free to discuss their questions or feelings with their parents.

Open and positive discussion lays the groundwork for trust between parent and child, and a healthy sense of self-esteem. Lie about the biological parents and the child may develop a need to lie in general; indicate that the biological parents are low people, and the child may develop a self-fulfilling prophecy that he will turn out the same way; avoid discussion and the child may conclude that there is something terribly wrong with his background or else he would have been told about it.

Children have an uncanny ability to sense when someone is lying or uncomfortable, but they have a narcissistic way of interpreting this information. They assume the lie or discomfort means there is something bad, wrong or unlovable about them.

One of the few real differences between adoptive and biological parenting is the need to help your child come to a healthy, positive acceptance that he has two sets of ancestors. It is more difficult for an adopted child to establish his sense of identity because of the very real fact that he has dual ancestry, but this is something that the vast majority of adoptees *can* understand and accept.

One study found only 8 percent of adoptees never accept the fact of their adoption and these were usually those who were not told about it early in life.[3] The vast majority of adoptees accept that their family was formed by adoption, but almost all children will question the facts surrounding their adoption frequently at various periods in their lives. "Telling" is not a single event, but a lifelong process.

Questioning origins does *not* indicate that your child does not love you. It is merely a natural curiosity that all people feel about where they came from and how they happened to be in this world. Children identify with the parents who raise and care for them, but they are still curious about genealogy.

Convey That Adoption Is a Natural Occurrence

It makes sense to most children that there are several ways parents can have children—either by bearing them or adopting them. (But it is important to let young children know they were originally born like everyone else.)

It also makes sense that some people can have babies, but not provide homes for them, while fate just causes other people to be good parents even though they cannot bear children. The older a child gets, the more he will realize that there is more to good parenting than just giving birth. Most are able to understand that the birth mother was not prepared for the responsibilities of parenthood, did not have enough money to support a baby, was too young to be a competent mother or wanted the baby to grow up in a home with both a mother and father to love him.

Convey a Positive Sense About the Birth Parents and the Fact That Adoption Was a Loving Choice

Research has found that one of the most damaging fears adoptees have is that they were rejected by the birth parents.[4] They want to know why the birth mother did not keep them and need reassurance that they were not given away because there was something "wrong" with them.

These fears can be calmed by your assurances that adoption is a difficult but loving decision birth mothers make. Studies have shown that most birth mothers do care deeply about having their baby grow up in homes that provide love, security and advantages.[5] One study found that less than 4 percent of birth mothers were callous about surrendering their babies.[6]

It is vital that you recognize and acknowledge this so that your child will not feel initially rejected. He needs this and other positive information about adoption to establish a good sense of self-esteem.

Not all your feelings about adoption will be positive, however. For example, Joan McNamara, an eloquent adoption advocate and parent has written, "One regret that both parents and children sometimes have is that the child was not born to the adoptive parents. This can be acknowledged so that together parents and child can share this small sadness. Part of being together is being able to share the good and bad. Once a fear or sad feeling is out in the open it can be accepted."[7] Children should be allowed to express any of their feelings about being adopted and to communicate openly about their background.

Collect Information for Your Child's Future Questions

Adoptees say they want to know that adoption was a loving choice made by the birth mother. They want as much information about their genealogy as possible. Plus many are curious about their birth parents' traits, talents and looks.

Collect as much information as possible about your child's biological parents and family background: nationality, education, health, physical appearance, occupations, talents and abilities. Information surrounding the actual birth (time and place of birth and type of delivery) and reasons for surrendering the child for adoption should be noted. Parents can share this information with their child when appropriate and when asked. If you did not get enough information before adoption, contact your agency and try to collect it now.

Some parents feel burdened by having such information, but this discomfort usually relates to a fear or feeling the parent has not adequately worked through. Does it reflect anger, resentment or moral indignation against the birth mother? Those parents who can empathize with the birth mother are more comfortable discussing adoption with their children and, thus, are more able to help their child build a positive self-image.

Are you afraid your child will discard you and search for his birth parents if you tell him about them? This is a widely held fear, but the truth seems to be the opposite. Children who have been able to find answers for their questions and have felt an open and comfortable attitude from their parents generally have less desire to search for their biological parents.

Telling Is Different for Each Case and for Each Age

What should you tell your child? There is no specific answer to this question, since each parent is facing a unique set of circumstances and feelings, but some guidelines can be given. In general, let the child pursue awareness of adoption at his own pace; tell him what he wants to know in terms he can understand, but no more than he wants to know. The most important things to convey are how much you wanted him, how much you love him now that you have him and how he is yours forever regardless of whatever happens.

Adoption is something that has to be explained in various ways at various ages. Small children can be overwhelmed by too many facts. Also, one explanation is not enough. There will be many questions, changing feelings and many misconceptions to unravel over the years.

It is often helpful, in each stage of your child's life, to have books about adoption for him to read. Librarians can supply such books or you can get a list of recommended books from Concerned Persons for Adoption, a nonprofit adoptive parents group.

They list books for adults and children, including ones that are appropriate for transracial and foreign adoptees. Send your request plus a stamped, self-addressed envelope to:

Concerned Persons for Adoption
200 Parsippany Road
Whippany, NJ 07981

Telling Your Baby

When you talk to your baby, when you feel like it, occasionally say something like "We're so glad we adopted you." He just needs to hear the word "adopted" said in a happy tone. One adult has happy memories of a tune her mother made up to rock her with, "my sweet little adopted baby."

Keep a photo album of pictures of you bringing your child home and of your family on the first day of adoption. This is a way of bringing the subject up in a natural and happy way, plus children always treasure and enjoy pictures and stories about themselves.

Questions from Age Three to Six

When your child asks "Where do babies come from?" merely tell him they grow in a special place inside a woman. He may ask if he grew inside you. It is hard to say he grew inside another woman, but do not brush his question off. You may even wish to initiate the conversation, when you are comfortable, if you see a pregnant woman.

It is a good idea to have your child know other adopted children, so he does not think being adopted is strange or unusual. Such social contact is one of the many benefits of joining an adoptive parents group.

Sooner or later he will ask, "Why didn't that lady want to keep me?" Tell him it's because she felt she couldn't give him a good home, but made a plan to find a Mommy and Daddy who would. Nothing more is needed at this time.

Middle Children, Age Six to Eleven

During this period, most children begin to wonder about their origins. Answer your child's questions as openly and as positively as you can. It is important to clarify any concerns he may have about adoption during this stage before he progresses to the more turbulent and emotional stage of adolescence.

Your child will probably question why he was not reared by his birth parents. Most seem able to understand the fact that the birth mother was not married and wanted a family with both a father and mother for the child. The difficulty she would face raising her child without a father seems like a good explanation to most children this age.

Adolescence, Age Twelve to Eighteen

Adolescence is a difficult time for children. Almost all teen-agers exhibit wide mood swings and make spiteful remarks to their parents. It is especially important during this stage to acknowledge the difference between adoptive and biological relationships, instead of having this be something else you and your teen-ager can fight about. On the other hand, always reaffirm that he is your own and your beloved child.

Your teen-ager may speak of his "real family" or question if he could be happier if he had stayed with his "real mother." He may be testing your feelings for him. He may also be testing how independent you will allow him to be. It is best to acknowledge that it is normal to wonder about things, but you can also say that while others are related to him biologically, you are his "real" family.

Teen-agers are especially prone to narcissistic views of life and to self-pity. Reading some books that deal with adoption can help them get perspective on the subject.

Adult Life

Questions and concerns about origins may be stimulated by any major life change such as going to college, going into the service, getting married or becoming a parent. Even filling out forms requesting background information can stir up questions. As with all children, it may not be until your child has children of his own that he will understand the special nature of the parenting and the love you gave him.

Your child's questioning *does not* indicate a desire to return to his biological parents, nor does it endanger his relationship with you. In fact, it is a tribute to his trust in you if he can freely question. By sharing ideas, feelings and discussions, your parent-child relationship will grow and deepen. His need to search for origins will probably lessen.

Some parents can enter these discussions without upset, while for others it is painful. Pearl Buck wrote of this when she said each period of questioning "must be met with love, and patience—and suffering. For the adoptive parents suffer too, not only for their child's sake but also for their own. There is a rending of the flesh and a breaking of the spirit when the child asks the cold question, 'Who am I? Why am I here?' But questions answered with warmth, openness and understanding provide the trust that binds you and your child into a lasting relationship."[8]

Special Situations

What if there is no information? Some children can accept this; others will be worried about any "bad" influences from their heritage. Or they will worry that they were rejected because of unknown "bad" causes. It is important to assure the child that you are sure his birth mother would have raised him if she could have, and that she must have cared about him because she made sure he found a family who would love him forever. It is also reassuring to tell him you know his birth parents must have been OK because there are so many good things about him.

In interracial or foreign adoption, your child and the community will be aware from an early age that family members have different heritages. Do not try to deny that difference, but point out the reality that different appearances have little to do with feelings of love. Your child can learn to feel good about the fact that he has positive influences from several heritages—adopted and biological.

Books about his racial or cultural heritage, trips to museums or the immigration exhibit at the Statue of Liberty can help instill a pride in all aspects of his ancestry. Adoptive parents groups can provide help, support and a feeling that there are other multicultural families around.

What about fears of "bad blood," especially if there are extremely negative facts in the child's background? Patricia J. Auth, Director of Adoption for Family Service of Westchester in White Plains, New York, says that even negative facts can be understood and accepted (1) if told at an appropriate age, (2) if asked for and (3) if told in a positive way. Many agencies will offer support in telling your child about such facts. Others will try to research information requested by adoptees and their families. Mrs. Auth, who helps families this way says, "We try to tell the child about the positive attributes of his birth parents. If there are negative facts, we tell them, but try to give an explanation of the life situation that caused these problems. For example, if the birth mother was promiscuous, and therefore the father is unknown, what led her to behave that way? Did she try to find love or self-esteem in such relationships?"

Telling Others

Most adoptees do not want their heritage discussed with relatives or others outside the family. It is not that they want adoption kept secret, but rather that they often want to control what is said about them.

Therefore, it is a good policy from the day you bring your child home to assure anyone who asks that the child has a "good background," but that it is family policy not to discuss any specifics. Obviously you will answer your pediatrician's questions about medical history, but some adoption advisers suggest making no mention of adoption to school officials. They fear having the child subjected to unfair prejudices and having problems magnified, as some claim happens to children of divorced parents. If problems occur in school, your child's concerns about adoption can be *one* of the many possible causative effects considered. But do be sure that your school has a policy of mentioning adoption in positive terms whenever course work on families is discussed.

Questions You Cannot Answer

In all probability your child will accept the fact that he was adopted, if you are comfortable with that fact. Most adoptees do. Some, often through no fault of their parents, develop fears and concerns and doubts. As Louise Raymond, an adoption worker and adoptive parent wrote, "The child who feels unloved or unworthy, whether he be biological or adopted, cannot rest as long as there is anything for him to be anxious about. If there seems to be nothing, he will find something. But the child who feels loved and worthwhile, biological or adopted, can . . .[accept]. . . his family's liabilities as well as its assets."[9]

It will probably be painful if you discover that your child has persistent questions that you cannot answer. He may develop the need to search for more information, or even to try and find his birth relatives. As discussed in the next chapter, you may wish to help your child find the answers he needs, because there is a good chance this will improve your relationship with him.

12

Searching for Origins

I was adopted by two very beautiful people. . . . They are the best . . . their love is priceless to me. But I always wonder about the blood that is in me and the people from where it came.

Adoptee, twenty-four years old

I never had any desire to search for my origins or even to know anything about them. I have no idea why I don't need to know, I just don't.

Adoptee, thirty-three years old

Finding my birth relatives was "cement" for me. It wasn't a happy experience, but it was a reality. I could drop the fantasies and go on from there. I don't know if my adopted parents believed it, but even when I was searching for my birth parents, they were my "forever" family. They raised me, they're my mom and daddy.

Adoptee, forty years old

Many parents live in fear that their child will go in search of his origins. They see a search as a rejection of the family life they offered. Even most of the active proponents of open records state that a search for heritage usually *does not* indicate a lack of love for adopted parents, *does not* indicate a lack of love in the adopted home and *does not* mean the adoptee is trying to find a new set of parents.[1] Most searching adoptees are being neither ungrateful nor unloving to their parents, but they have developed deeply troubling questions about themselves and their heritage. If your child develops a need to search you may want to help, believe it or not.

Almost all adoptees identify with their adoptive parents, but this identification does not mean that many, at some time or another, will not want information about their ancestry. Some will want more. Their curiosity or doubts will not be satisfied until they meet their blood relatives.

How many have that need? Some activists claim that every adoptee dreams of being reconciled with his birth parents. This clearly isn't true. No records are kept in the United States, since there is no central place where adoptees can gain access to their records. In Scotland, however, adult adoptees can apply to Register House for their original birth certificates. One ten-year study[2] found that each year in Scotland an average of 1.5 adult adoptees per 1,000 requested such information. Sixty percent of those searchers wanted to meet their birth parents, the rest merely wanted more information on heritage. Even adoptees who want to meet their birth parents usually want information; or want to meet in order to find what they look like or to ask why they were placed for adoption.

This chapter is *not* written to take sides in the controversy over whether or not adoption records should be sealed, nor will the chapter debate a birth mother's right to privacy vs. an adoptee's right to information. It is written to explain to parents why some adoptees need to search for more information and why it is not as threatening as it seems at first. Perhaps the words of one adoptee can explain some of the feelings that can lead to a search: "I am sixty-one years old and I would still like to know what sort of family I come from—what kind of national origin, what kind of people they were—and did this affect my personality? I had six children and each time there was the fear that maybe there was something unhealthy in my background that would show up when they were born.

"My parents loved me and I loved them. They told me I was adopted but they found it impossible to concede that I ever had a past they did not share. They had a great need to have me as a person with no separate background. I agreed I was their child, but I didn't agree that I shared their family background. I felt part of my individuality was being denied.

"The tension was so intense that when I secured my birth certificate for a passport at age twenty-one, I never sought to find out more about my origins until both parents died. They are dead now and I suppose I will never know.

"I have resented the sentimental, unrealistic picture of a child's 'reunion' with his 'real' or 'biological' mother. I have equally resented the contention that adoptive parents by virtue of their love for the child are the child's only parents. They don't have to destroy the beginning to have the child. I feel badly that everyone conspired to do that to me. I just had a genealogical need—that's all."

The Reasons Adoptees Search

There are many reasons why adoptees search, but one adoption social worker who has worked with many adoptees claims that at the base of most searches there lies the questions, "Is there something wrong with me? Is there something wrong with my heritage?" There is often the fear that he was surrendered for adoption because of some unknown defect in himself or his family.

Many people, adopted and biological, grow up with the feeling there is something wrong with them or that they do not fit in with their family or community. Most people wonder "Who am I? Where did I come from?" An adoptee often believes there may be an answer in his biological origins.

Sometimes these fears develop when the child is not told about adoption in a positive way. The Scottish study,[3] which is important for its comprehensive sample, found that most of the searchers, especially those who wanted to meet their birth parents, had been told about adoption at a late date, usually after they were ten. Many parents refused to give information about the birth parents and would not discuss adoption. Those who would discuss the birth parents, usually did so in a negative way. Over 80 percent of these searchers had very low self-images, but not all searchers have low self-esteem or bad experiences with being told.

For many, it is the lack of concrete information that breeds doubts, uncertainty and conflict. They feel, like Betty Jean Lifton, who wrote, "I wanted myth and reality to merge, to know who I came from, what blood was in my veins. I wanted to live consciously, to get rid of the confusion and chaos cluttering my mind. To be real."[4] As long as there were unknowns for Lifton, she writes that she did not know "whether to feel deprived of this 'real identity' or lucky to have escaped it."[5] Adoptees who feel like this, only know that they must find the answers if they are to achieve peace.

Other adoptees become obsessed by the fear that there may be some defective genes or inherited disease that they are carrying. If such fears are present they are made more urgent by a pregnancy.

Many have the desire to know whether there are any brothers and sisters or even half-brothers and sisters. The desire to meet these siblings is often stronger than the desire to meet the birth parents.

Perhaps the main reason that parents are afraid of these questions is the mistaken belief that if the adoptee felt like their child, he would not ask such questions. Many parents feel questions indicate a lack of love toward them. As Ann Carney, a parent by adoption, writes: "They are giving him love and security, bed and board, plus a legal name that guarantees him rights of inheritance and guardianship. In return they want his love as a member of the family."[6]

Some adoptees, a very small percent, are searching for loving parents. Like any group of parents, some adopters are cruel or cold, but this is not true of all the parents of adoptees wanting to reunite in a loving parental relationship with birth relatives. Some of these searchers have developed an unrealistic dislike for their parents, and often only a meeting with birth parents can dispel these feelings.

Children must learn to cope with the reality that parents can be loving sometimes and angry at others; that the parent who buys treats is also the parent who disciplines. Instead of accepting this duality, some children decide that they must have been adopted away from all-kind, all-loving parents. Most children eventually accept the reality of human nature and responsible parenting, but it can be harder for adoptees to give up the fantasy of all-good parents lost in the past. Perhaps those who cannot give up this fantasy are those who resent discipline more than others. But most give it up when they meet their birth parents and fantasy comes hard up against reality. Most searchers, however, merely want information or to meet the birth relatives, not to establish another parent-child relationship.

Ignoring the questions or getting angry at the curiosity will not make the desire to search go away. Eighty-year-old adoptees can still be obsessed with the questions they wanted answered as children. Most love their adopted parents but resent any obstacles that were put in the way of their search.

Is It Sick to Search?

Some mental health professionals and agency officials believe that searchers are neurotic and express some disturbance. Some studies have shown that it is the more poorly adjusted adoptees who search for more information or a meeting with their birth parents,[7] but this is not always so. Co-founders of the Adoption Research Project in Los Angeles, Sorosky, Baran and Pannor, studied a group of American searchers and concluded that even adoptees from the most loving and nurturing homes, even those who had never suffered any traumatic experiences, even those with good relationships with parents and peers, sometimes developed the need to search.[8] Why? In part it seems to vary with the temperament and innate curiosity of each adoptee.

Each of us gains our sense of identity from several sources, such as our personality, beliefs, feelings, family, environment and genealogy. Each person seems to put different importance on the various factors and no one knows why some people are more bothered than others by a lack of genealogical information. Some psychoanalysts say that for any adoptee who seriously asks about his past, such information is a prerequisite for his future development.[9]

Should You Help Your Child Search?

Many parents initially feel rejected if they find their child has the desire to search for more information on his biological origins, or especially if he wants to find birth relations. Many feel this indicates ingratitude for all they have given their child. If they are sensitive and see that the desire to search reflects a deep and painful need in their child, parents often lose their hurt or anger.

The main reason the adoptive parents fight a search is the fear that a meeting will take place and they will lose their child to his original parents. This fear was found to some degree in *every* parent interviewed by Sorosky, Baran and Pannor.[10] Some said even the mention of a search made them feel like they had merely been a caretaker or baby-sitter for their child.

In fact, the relationship between adoptive parents and children seems almost always to be enhanced by the search,[11] especially if the adoptive parents are supportive. Most adoptees, however, are afraid to tell their parents that they want to search. They fear hurting the parents or losing their love. It is a relief when parents understand and accept the adoptee's yearning for information.

If the relationship has been good between parent and adoptee, it usually gets better once the search begins. If the relationship has been strained, it is rarely made worse. In fact, the repressed curiosity or worry over origins is often the factor that has weakened the bond between parents and child. An adoptee who holds the fantasy that birth parents are more loving than the adoptive parents usually gains a new and more positive perspective on his family. He often feels for the first time that his adoptive parents are his *real* parents. As Sorosky, Baran and Pannor concluded, "One of the striking aftereffects of reunions (between adoptees and birth parents) was the enhancement of the relationship between adoptees and their adoptive parents."[12]

The question, therefore, is usually not whether or not to fight the search, but how much to help. The answer in part has to do with the age of the adoptee. If he is under eighteen, most experts believe a meeting is inadvisable.[13] Adolescence is too confusing a time to be faced with two sets of parents in the flesh. Thus, it is usually best only to help an adolescent adoptee express his feelings, clarify his goals and obtain any non-identifying information he can.

Researchers say that most adolescent adoptees do not want to find their birth parents anyway. They are merely curious about aspects of their background.[14] Consciously or unconsciously, they are usually asking for reassurance that they are loved and wanted in their family. They also want to know that there is nothing "wrong" with them.

If an adoptee wants to contact his birth relatives, most counselors suggest you not try to stop anyone who is over eighteen. They also suggest that you allow the adoptee to do most of the work himself. Some will drop the whole project if they do not meet with parental resistance. Others will appreciate their parents' understanding and acceptance, since most adoptees are afraid their parents will reject them if they want to search.

How to Search

The first step is to contact the agency or go-between who arranged the adoption. While some will refuse to share any information, even if it is available, many others believe that a heartfelt need for information should be answered, especially if the adoptive parents give their approval. In some cases, agencies will even contact birth parents and arrange a meeting, if all parties agree.

If the agency or go-between is unable or unwilling to help, one of the adoption search support groups may be able to assist. The group in your state is probably the best source of information on the current status of birth records, where such records are kept, what court is in charge of unsealing records and what methods have been most successful in tracking the information desired. These facts differ by state and can change from year to year. Your state official in charge of adoption (see Appendix A) should be able to give you this information also, plus the names of any adoptee support groups nearby. NACAC (see p. 28) will also supply a list of adoption search support groups.

The various groups provide different levels of assistance. Some maintain reunion files, some actively assist in searches and others merely offer moral support. Some adoptees and their parents find that by attending meetings held by such organizations, they come to a better understanding of the interrelated situations of all the parties involved in adoption. Old resentments and fears can be soothed and fears regarding a search can be shared with others who may have similar feelings.

If agencies or go-betweens cannot provide the desired information, most searchers try to track their birth relatives. This type of search usually begins by obtaining a copy of the original birth certificate. It often contains the names and addresses of the birth parents and grandparents at the time of birth. Some states will supply the original birth certificate to adults who request it and pay the small required fee. In other states a court order is necessary to "unseal" these records. Courts and individual judges vary in their willingness to unseal records.

Such records have only been sealed for about forty years. They were closed by reformers who believed it was damaging for adoptees to have different birth certificates from other children. So they arranged for the original birth certificate with the birth parents' names, or "father unknown" or "illegitimate" stamped on it to be sealed away, and a new one issued with the names of the adopting parents printed on it. Birth certificates were also sealed to prevent the birth mother from intruding on the parents and child, and vice versa.

Once the original birth certificate is obtained, there are various detective methods that adoptees have used to track down their biological origins. Adoption search support groups such as the Adoptees Liberty Movement Association (ALMA) (P.O. Box 154, Washington Bridge Station, New York, NY 10033) are the best source of the latest methods and legal changes.

What Will Be Found?

The main fear is that "awful truths" will be found. What if the adoptee finds out his mother was a prostitute, his father was a murderer or that schizophrenia runs in the family? Sorosky, Baran and Pannor state, "Such potentially traumatic revelations can occur and pose a risk to the searching adoptee. However, since most adoptees have had such fantasies, they may also be in a better position to deal with such realities than we heretofore assumed."[15] They researched meetings where "awful truths" were discovered and concluded that even these searches and reunions were usually treated in a positive way by the adoptee, who, with answered questions, could get on with living his life.

Studies show the vast majority of adoptees will not find anything overwhelmingly negative in their origins.[16] Searchers usually find that they had birth mothers with very good and caring reasons for not keeping their babies. Most adopters will find they were born illegitimate, that their birth parents knew each other for a while, cared about each other, but did not feel able to provide a stable home or marriage for the child.[17] If searchers meet or speak with their birth mother, they tend to find a woman who remembers their birthday every year, who wonders how life turned out for them and who wants the child to know the reasons he was surrendered for adoption.

What the adoptee will probably *not* find is a birth parent who wants to act as a real parent. While there may be some, Sorosky, Baran and Pannor found *none* of the birth parents in their sample who desired a meeting envisioned developing a parental relationship with the adoptee. The birth parents they studied were grateful to the adoptive parents for raising the child and had no desire to hurt or interfere. Eighty-seven percent regarded the adoptive parents as the "real" parents.[18]

While many adoptees who want a meeting with birth parents envision being received with open arms, this is not usually what happens. Furthermore, most adoptees who meet their birth parents find that they have very little in common with them.[19] But this is a truth that an adoptee wanting a reunion must discover for himself. He would probably resent any parent who tried to squelch his search by telling him these things.

The study of Scottish adoptees[20] revealed that about 80 percent were glad they had found their birth records and the information contained. (Time and place of birth, parents' names and occupations, address at time of birth, name of grandparents.) They may not have found information they considered positive, but it dispelled questions that had troubled them. This is the experience reported by most adoptees who find the information they seek. Studies[21] have also shown that the adoptive relationship usually improves sooner or later after a successful search. Adoptees drop their fantasies about all-good birth parents, or fears about themselves, and are often able to see the love they were given through the years by their parents. They can offer these parents a less troubled affection.

Unfortunately, some adoptees find that once answers are found, their troubles do not disappear. Their problems are due to personality or life situations, not adoption issues. At least a search will usually help clarify what is wrong so that corrective measures can be taken.

13

Handling Upsetting Remarks

How did we ever get him? He's not like us at all.
Father's comment overheard by his five-year-old

You're not my real mother! My real mother is beautiful and kind.
Angry seven-year-old to her mother

Everyone that meets her asks her where she gets her eyes.
Dark-eyed parents about their blue-eyed daughter

Situations like these are unsettling. They stir up feelings of not belonging. Such incidents cause adoptive families to explain themselves and justify their relationships. These comments, however, were all reported by biological parents.

All families have to deal with differences and have to cope with unthoughtful comments. Adoptive families, however, have the additional burden of dealing with a whole set of prejudices in our society held by people who view adoption as an inferior or uncomfortable way of forming a family. Sociologist David Kirk[1] identified some of those prejudices. He found 56 percent of the people he polled believed there was more risk to adopting than having a biological child. Studies have shown that there is no negative difference between adopted and non-adopted children, but only 30 percent of Kirk's sample said there was equal risk. Children are screened by pediatricians and professionals before they are offered for adoption, and prospective parents are warned of any problems before they assume responsibility, but only 6 percent of people acknowledged this by saying there was less risk in adopting.

Kirk also found that many people expect a parent to care more for a biological than adopted child. This study was conducted in the 1950s, but parents still encounter many of the same forms of prejudice today when they adopt.

Where do people get these prejudices? In part from the media. Adoptees are often portrayed as troubled individuals. Often they are seen searching for birth parents or engaging in loving meetings with their biological families. As stated before, these stories represent a small minority of adoptees. The more representative stories about the overwhelmingly positive aspects of adoption are apparently not dramatic enough for the media to feature.

More subtle examples of media prejudice involve the obituaries that note which surviving children are adopted, as if that makes a difference. More insidious, when a major crime is committed by someone who was adopted, that irrelevant fact is usually mentioned. Adoptees are no more criminally inclined than anyone else, but the mention of adoption leaves a negative impression. The mention of any somewhat unusual fact would stay in people's minds. If the press always mentioned when a criminal had a protruding bellybutton, the public would soon develop prejudices about "outies."

To get more psychological, prejudices can arise because adoption is threatening to some people. For example, many parents have the occasional, fleeting desire to give away their children. These thoughts are kept secret because they are unacceptable. Adoption can create discomfort in people whose desires to be rid of their children are strong but upsetting. Adoption occurs when birth parents give up their children; but the motive is usually loving, not hostile. To cope with their own temptations, some people with hostile feelings toward their children have to criticize adoption.

Similarly, some parents do not think of their children as treasures. Yet adoption confronts them with other people who go to great effort and often great expense to acquire children. This discrepancy in values creates discomfort.

Then there are the people who draw distinctions between adoptees and "your own" children. One person said to a father, in front of his son, "I could never feel an adopted child was my own." The father stifled his anger and replied in a neutral tone, "Some can, some can't. No one should adopt if they can't. But I certainly feel my son is my own."

You will be asked if your child is "your own." Even worse, one mother reports she is occasionally asked, "Do you have any children of your own?" while she is with her Vietnamese son. "Yes, him," she replies. He may have different genes, but he is legally and emotionally her own.

People will seek you out and ask you about your adoption experiences. They will want to know how they can adopt. They will also ask how you handle the issues surrounding two heritages. You will have to decide what you want to share and what you want to keep private.

You and your children have a right to privacy, and you do not have to answer questions that make you uncomfortable. To any question you can reply, "We have chosen not to discuss anything like that outside the family."

On the other hand, since adoption was a happy event, it is an experience you would probably like to help other people share. Where do you draw the line between someone asking for help and someone who is being nosy or intrusive?

Most people are comfortable talking about the methods they used to adopt and any problems they had to overcome to adopt. Many think that anything that regards their child's heritage or current family problems is private. Talk these issues over in your family. When your child is old enough, tell him you want to help others find the happiness that you have found through adoption, and ask if he minds your talking about his adoption. Many children do not like to be talked about publicly, and they often do not like anything discussed in front of friends that makes them different from the crowd. Your child will probably not want his adoption discussed in the middle of the supermarket, but probably would not mind your offering to take prospective adopters to an adoptive parents group meeting or privately discussing adoption methods with them in your home.

Your child may wish to use the technique known in the field as "the cover story" to handle questions about where he came from. The story should be (1) short, (2) basically true, (3) positive and (4) developed by both parents and child. An example is: "My birth mother was sick (unspecified illness) for a long time or was too young to be a mother, so she decided to give me the opportunity to have a real family of my own. My parents wanted a child and applied to an agency and God (or fate or luck) brought us together." Of course, you and your child may decide merely to answer any such questions with, "We don't discuss that; it's private."

Gossip

What about gossip or teasing in the neighborhood? Some adoptees have been deeply hurt by gossip about their adoption or illegitimacy. It is important for your child to know that he can bring home any gossip—or any problem—and discuss it with you. Home should be a place to go for support, a place to gain strength for facing the world, a place where any concern can be openly discussed. This instills a strong sense of family, and that is a great asset for any child. You must let him know that you are not afraid to hear anything that is said about him.

By seeing you dispute or dismiss gossip, your child will tend to learn the same ability. Part of the growth of self-esteem in anyone involves gaining pride in oneself and the ability to defend against the cruel words of others.

There are numerous examples of adoptees turning verbal attacks to their own advantage. The basis of a good defense for your child lies in his knowledge of how much you wanted him and how pleased you are to have him. This is not to suggest you overemphasize that he was a "chosen" child; that story leads to too many shattered feelings when adoptees discover they were not selected in a baby supermarket. Although you did not personally choose your child out of a group (except if you chose him from a photo-listing book), you certainly chose to adopt him. He should know this.

You had to work harder to be a parent than most people who form their family biologically. You got to know him, had to make the decision to have him as part of the family and then go to court to request permission to do so. No child comes to a family through adoption by mistake or by accident—adoption is the most planned parenthood possible. Your child was wanted by you, and he should know it. Telling your child this, and often mentioning how happy you are to have him, will help him form the security he needs to dismiss gossip.

How to handle comments about the birth mother who "gave the child away"? Your child will wonder about this and you may be asked about it by others. One mother says she is often asked, "How could anyone abandon a beautiful child like that?" The child, in fact, had been abandoned at an orphanage door in South America. In most such cases, the mother was very poor and knew she could not feed or clothe her baby properly. Most of these mothers, in great anguish, leave the child with people who will care for him and find him a good home. Perhaps abandoning mothers fear that any questioning by the orphanage would weaken their resolve.

The vast majority of birth mothers studied do not give up their children lightly.[2] It is usually a well-considered decision made with the welfare of the child in mind. The birth mother does not want the pain of illegitimacy or poverty for her child, or she realizes that she is not ready to assume the responsibility of parenthood at this time, and both she and her child would suffer if she tried. It is very important to recognize that making an adoption plan for a child can be as equally loving a decision as raising a child.

You can use these facts to help explain adoption to your child and others, but you do not have to lecture. One mother heard her small daughter say, "My first mother didn't want me." The child had been abused, and the mother could have gone into a lengthy explanation of the personal problems that can lead to abuse—she will one day—but that day, she merely hugged her child and said, "Well, you sure have a mommy who wants you now."

Transracial Insults

Transracial adopters face special problems. One mother expecting a South American baby heard a friend complain, "You have to watch these Spanish housekeepers. You can't leave any money out around them." She firmly but pleasantly replied, "You know, my baby is of Spanish heritage and I don't want her growing up hearing things like that."

Dorothy DeBolt, mother and founder of AASK, an organization to support special needs adoption, reported a more vicious incident after she adopted a black child.[3] An anonymous telephone caller asked to speak to Mrs. Nigger Lover. Dorothy replied, "This is she. What can I do for you?" The DeBolt's are so relaxed about their interracial family that when they meet with an incredulous "Is *that* your daughter?" Bob DeBolt has been known to reply, "Yes, do you think she looks like her mother or me?"

You and your child will simply have to face the fact that there is racial prejudice and adoption prejudice in this world. As long as you are secure in your love and admiration for each other, you will know that the people with prejudice are wrong and you are right. Even though one study found that 50 percent of children in black/white adoptions had encountered some form of social cruelty, the researchers found it did not affect their adjustment or their relationships with others.[4]

A mother of a bi-racial child helped him cope with a teasing classmate by saying, "There are a lot of people who don't understand—who have limited vision. You will just have to understand and accept this." Then she told him, "I didn't always feel like I fit in either, when I was a child." They discussed feelings of being different—feelings that almost every person as a child feels, but considers uniquely awful. After this talk the child was better able to understand himself and his mother, and to cope with the problem.

Some families never encounter prejudice until their child starts dating. One mother of a Korean teen-ager was shocked when his girl friend's parents objected to their relationship. Of course those things will hurt both you and your child. The task is to find a constructive way to deal with those feelings.

Comments About Appearance

Differences in appearance, even less dramatic than transracial ones, can cause discomfort. One set of short parents, for example, were troubled by the fact that their tall son was always asked where he got his height. He would quickly, and they felt defensively, reply that he was adopted. Perhaps if they discussed this with their son and asked if such questions made him uncomfortable, they could discover whether the discomfort lay in them or their child. If questions upset the child, why? Is it reminding him of other fears he has about his heritage? Perhaps those fears can be researched. Is it merely his discomfort with the physical differences? He has a right to make any reply he wants. For example, an equally accurate, but more private answer might be "Some of my relatives were tall, but my parents are short." Adoption is nothing to hide, but no one need wear it as a badge either.

Remarks From the Family

Some of the most hurtful remarks don't come from outsiders, they come from the family. David Kirk found that 20 percent of prospective grandparents disapproved of adoption plans.[5] The disapproval rate was much higher if the adopters had biological children. Disapproval is also initially high in transracial adoptions. One prospective grandparent of an Indian baby said, "Why are you exposing two perfectly beautiful children [his biological grandchildren] to this?"

Of course you would be angry in that situation! But if you control your anger and explain your motives, most grandparents will come around. Kirk found that 95 percent did.[6] Their secret fear may be that you are doing this to spite them. It will be important for you to stress your love for the grandparents and your desire for them to love your new child.

What if they do not come around? What if they continue to be cold to your child or to actively play favorites with your biological child? Give them some time and encouragement to warm up. Explain your distress. If they cannot change, you may have to make the visits short and infrequent. In severe cases, you may have to end the relationship, but this is rare.

Some of the most unsettling comments come from your children. You will have to be so secure in your love for your child and so relaxed about the reality of your own parenthood that you can handle these remarks with a minimum amount of upset.

For example, if you adopt an older child, one who remembers his birth parents or foster parents, he may want to visit them or he may talk positively about them. This can make his new parents feel unloved or unappreciated. His talk about his former parents will probably diminish as his security in his relationship with you grows. He may have to idealize them for a while until he is sure he is accepted by you.

Some adoptees feel disloyal when they begin to love their new parents. Your best response is to try to assure your child that his birth parents would be happy that he found a nice home and new parents to love him forever. One boy imagined his birth mother visiting his new home and being pleased. Another had to actually go and see his old home before he could settle into his new one.[7]

Alfred Kadushin, who studied older adoptees, reports that only 5 percent of them retained feelings about birth parents that interfered with the adoptive relationship.[8] He advises that excessive talk of birth parents is a phase that will pass; parents must be confident enough in the ultimate positive outcome and have the "strength to make the most difficult of responses; not responding at all."

It isn't just older adoptees who can make hurtful remarks, children adopted at birth can do it, too. David Kirk[9] has written of two poignant examples. A boy insisted on finding out his birth mother's name and claimed he was going to take it as his legal name when he was old enough. His father empathized with him for having his name taken away against his will, but said that names show where we belong. Therefore, he said, if his son insisted on changing his name when older, the name would be added to the family name, so they could continue to belong together. Understood and accepted in such a loving way, the issue ceased to be important to the boy. If the father had become furious about the boy's ungrateful behavior, the issue probably would have stayed alive.

Similarly, a daughter said in anger to her mother, "I bet my other mommy was prettier than you and better than you." The mother answered, "I'm sure she was beautiful, because you are. I don't know if she was better, but I'll at least admit to the possibility." By not becoming defensive, she defused the situation. She and the daughter laughed at her comeback.

No one feels like laughing when their child says, "I hate you. I don't want to live with you anymore." You must know that biological parents have the same thing said to them in anger. Such statements are upsetting to any parent, but they can be especially threatening to a family formed by adoption. Has the child a legitimate complaint; have you been too harsh on him or too demanding? Or is he the kind of child who tends to fly off the handle initially to any form of discipline. In many of these cases, regardless of the circumstances, what the child is *really* saying is, "I'm afraid you hate me. I'm afraid you do not want me anymore." Reassure the child of your love while trying to help him learn to communicate in a more direct and positive manner.

A relaxed, nondefensive approach on your part usually takes away the anger and the importance from upsetting remarks. But this is not always the case. What if neighbors continue to gossip or continue vicious teasing? Perhaps you may have to move. What if your child continues to be troubled or troublesome about adoption issues? This can be an indication of the need for professional help. Counseling may not be necessary, but in cases where it is needed, it can make all the difference. Ask your adoptive parents group or agency to recommend a counselor with adoption experience. He can help work through any issues that are keeping you from feeling like a family.

14

Overcoming Problems

Adopted children do not have additional emotional and social problems just because they are adopted, but . . . they will have severer problems if vital situations bring a reaction of fear or anxiety from significant adults in their environment.[1]

Anna Elonen and Edward Schwartz
Adoption Researchers

Adoptive parents tend to overreact to their child's expression of aggressive and sexual feelings. . . . Adoptive parents tend to speak of heredity of children as major causative factors in any behavior difficulty that develops.[2]

Arthur Sorosky, Annette Baran and Reuben Pannor
Co-founders of the Adoption Research Project in Los Angeles

All kids are going to have some behavior problems some of the time. Almost every child will occasionally lie; steal; play with matches; act rebellious, aggressive, nervous or lazy. Didn't you?

Most parents when faced with such behavior are going to wonder what's the best way to handle the problem. Should they ignore the problem, discuss it or impose discipline? Obviously, the correct response varies with the situation, but two general rules can be applied. First, try and decide how serious the problem is. Second, try and determine what is causing it.

How do you tell how serious the problem is? First check child development books and see if the behavior is typical for your child's age. Perhaps your child is at an age or stage where it is normal for a child to behave in a difficult manner.

In some stages children normally feel more easygoing and secure. Then, as the child grows into another stage and has to cope with growth spurts, new social tasks or hormonal changes, his behavior may turn worse. He may seem tense, irritable or withdrawn. Some stages can be so frustrating that any parent can wonder why they ever left their childless state.

Everyone has heard of the "terrible two's"—that period when two year olds seem only to throw tantrums and yell "No!" But many parents haven't heard that almost every age and stage has some typical type of "bad" behavior along with the loveable.

It's normal, for example, for five and six year olds to be fascinated with "dirty words" and to want to play show and tell with their bodies. It is equally normal for a fourteen-year-old to have a telephone permanently attached to his ear and to groan "Oh, mother!" suddenly deciding that parents are hopelessly gauche.

You certainly may want to limit or modify such behavior, but you need not worry excessively about any behavior that is age-appropriate. As one mother said, "My three year old was so happy and sweet, but when she turned three and a half she suddenly became extremely irritable and demanding. I was tearing my hair out until I read the Gesell Institute books[3] assuring me it would pass when she became four."

If you know what is normal behavior at each stage and what sort of behavior problems are normal too, there is less chance of overreacting or underreacting. The parent who adopts especially needs this information so that behavior is not unfairly attributed to poor heredity or adoption problems.

The good news is that each stage may pass in six months or a year with luck and some help from you. The bad news is that some stages are pretty rough on parents, especially if they take you by surprise. Some parents will find it easy to handle the passive stages (or a child with a generally passive personality), while other parents are more comfortable with the more outgoing, even rebellious, ones.

If after checking the child development books, you are still concerned, confidentially ask the advice of someone familiar with children—parents of an older child, members of your adoptive parents group or a teacher. Your school psychologist or social worker may be helpful. You don't want to talk about your child too much behind his back, but you do want to get an idea of whether or not you are overreacting. You also want to know how other parents handled similar problems.

Try to understand why your child is behaving this way. If you can determine the motive, you may be able to help him get what he wants in a more positive way.

His behavior may be a reflection of his personality or temperament (see Part III, chapter 10) that you can modify. On the other hand, your child may be reacting to some upsetting event. Has anything happened recently to cause distress? Has a new baby arrived, or has anything else happened to make the child feel insecure? Has he had problems with his friends? Have you been giving him too much or too little attention or discipline? Have you and your spouse been fighting lately? Anxiety over problems in the family or problems with peers can affect a child's behavior.

If there are no other probable causes, question whether your child's problems may be a reaction caused by some anxiety he has developed concerning adoption. Your child may have become worried about his biological heritage—worried something is "wrong" with him. He may have begun to feel secretly angry at his birth parents for "deserting" him, and this unrealistic anger may be displaced on adoptive parents unless it is worked through. On the other hand, some adoptees become worried that their parents will "give them away" if they are bad (a fantasy they develop to explain their birth parents' decision) so the adoptees act "bad" to see if their parents will reject them.

This all sounds complicated and confusing. It is. Sometimes you need professional help to straighten it out, because children can't always tell you why they are behaving in a difficult way. A child who is being troublesome to get attention, for example, would not be able to tell you his motive because it is unconscious. He would merely be unwittingly seeking more love while behaving in an unloveable manner.

You can be sure that if your child's behavior leaves you baffled and frustrated, something is causing it. You can also be sure that if you are beginning to label your child "bad" or "lazy" or in some other negative way, you had better stop now. Children have a way of continuing to behave like the labels they are given.

School Problems

The only difference studies have found when comparing groups of adopted and nonadopted children is that adopted children seem to have more learning problems.[4] One study found that while adoptees are equal to the general population in terms of the level of education they attained, 47 percent seemed to be underachievers in terms of their own abilities.[5]

Several theories have been suggested for the learning problems, and each is probably right for some cases. Some have suggested that parents may be setting standards that are too high for their children to meet. Thus, they discourage their children from trying. Others suggest learning blocks are psychological and develop in reaction to learning too late in childhood about adoption or to frustration over a lack of knowledge about origins.

A more simple explanation may be found if adoptees are tested for learning disabilities. A child with learning disabilities has an average or above-average IQ. He is smart, but seems unable to learn or perform as well as he should because of subtle neurological problems or developmental learning lags. These problems are usually outgrown or compensated for by adulthood, but people with learning disabilities often underachieve or feel stupid because they have mysterious and frustrating trouble learning.

Why suspect adoptees of having a greater incidence of learning disabilities than the general population? Because learning disabilities are often caused by a long or difficult birth. Adoptees are often the first children of teen-age birth mothers; teen-agers and women having their first child are more likely to experience long and difficult births. Thus, adoptees should be tested for learning disabilities before they are labeled underachievers or psychologically blocked.

Discipline

Just because some forms of "bad" behavior are normal for some ages or may be caused by underlying anxieties does not mean that you should not impose limits or discipline to change this behavior. For example, one normally polite child began to insult his parents when he was eleven. His parents knew he was upset over the loss of a friend, plus they read that it was not unusual for eleven year olds to express sudden bursts of anger. The father said, "I guess we can expect to have to live with this throughout the teen years." But the mother said that she wouldn't tolerate being insulted by her friends and she certainly wasn't going to accept it from her son.

The parents agreed to set limits on the way their child could express his anger. (It is vital for parents to agree on such actions, otherwise they will undermine each other.) They told their son that if he had a complaint, he could talk it over with them, but insults were not allowed. He would be denied TV privileges any day he insulted his parents.

The boy was happier when the insults were stopped. Children know when they are out of line, and it makes them uncomfortable, even though they will often continue until they are stopped.

One family counselor specializing in adoption said, "Discipline is the hardest thing for parents who adopt. They seem to feel they don't have the right to be authoritative. Somehow, underneath, they feel they did not birth the child, therefore, they should not discipline the child. I work with good people who are good parents, but if they do not set limits, the child takes advantage and that can wreck a family."

Do not be afraid to set house rules and to speak up if your child is being destructive or inconsiderate. Children have to be taught to obey rules, and it does not come automatically to them. If the rules are fair, and if they are enforced in a firm, consistent and noninsulting manner, children generally do not mind. In fact, children may fuss, but they expect to have to follow rules.

Your child needs limits, structure and discipline for several reasons. First, it is important to teach a child that actions have consequences. Praise and privileges are earned by good behavior. Displeasure and limited privileges for "bad" behavior. This is the way you help your child develop a conscience and a style that helps him get along with other people. Second, children need to learn to control their impulses, and you will have to help them learn this even when they are adolescents.

Finally, children know at a deep level that a parent who is truly comfortable in the role and truly loves them will be able to discipline. As one adult adoptee said, "My parents were really great but I never quite felt like I belonged. They were never as hard on me as they were on the other (biological) kids."

Overindulgence and lack of discipline is not love. It is an abdication of parental responsibility. If you do not know how to discipline, there are books to help.

Books on child behavior and child development can suggest ways to handle problems. But do not be intimidated by "expert" opinion. Experts disagree on the best methods, so the most important thing is for parents to develop a disciplinary style of their own.

Family Problems

Many adoptees are only children, and "onlies" are often accused of being selfish and troubled. Recent studies have disputed these myths and shown "onlies" to be no more maladjusted or self-centered than anyone else.[6] In fact they are more likely to be intelligent and leaders than children with siblings.

Being a parent of an only child can be difficult. Every child-rearing incident is a new experience. This can make a parent somewhat nervous and overprotective. One of the reasons only children are, as a group, more intelligent than others is that they get so much parental attention. This can be carried to the extreme by parents who become overly focused on their child. The parents of an only child must make sure that both they and their child have friends and interests outside the nuclear family.

If there is more than one child in the home, there can be concern about sibling rivalry. Of course there will be jealousy and rivalries between siblings—that's normal. Sometimes it does not show for a year or more. Sometimes it is shown by excessive concern instead of hostility. Parents must tread a thin line—acknowledging to their children that jealousy is normal while praising cooperation and not allowing cruelty.

If one of the siblings is biological and one adopted, there can be some accusation of preferential treatment to one or the other. But you run this risk even if both children are biological or adopted. If one child takes extreme and continued offense, it may have more to do with their temperament than with actual injustice. Of course, though, you should thoroughly consider whether or not you are playing favorites.

There are those who claim adoptees are more prone to separation anxiety and thus are more vulnerable to death, divorce or remarriage in their family. One study[7] comparing groups of adoptees and nonadoptees found that these incidents arouse insecurities in all children. They found adoptees to be no more affected than others. All children will be upset by these events and it is important to prepare them and monitor their reactions.

One recent divorcée said her children were doing fine—at least as fine as could be expected. No extra trauma was evident because they were adopted. The parents had firmly agreed that whatever their problems, they were going to keep cordial relations for the children's sake. They assured the children of their continuing love and involvement, and each continued to live in the children's school district to minimize disruptions and maximize their availability to the children. With this sort of effort and cooperation, the children should not be unduly damaged by divorce. One study found that over a third of *all* children are still depressed about their parents' divorce five years after the fact.[8] But this seems to be a result of the parents' lack of acceptance of the divorce or the fact that one parent had virtually abandoned the children, plus the lack of a strong personality in the child prior to the divorce.

Some adoptees do have special problems with abandonment fears (some nonadoptees do, too). On one hand, you will have to be sensitive to hear if there is any special adoption issues that your child is struggling with, for example the fear that he was unloveable and therefore given up by his birth mother and again by divorced relatives. On the other hand, you will not want to see problems that are not there. Problems that occur often have more to do with the child's temperament or the parents' own adjustment than with the fact of adoption.

An Adoption That Is Not Working

Problems that develop should be handled as in any family. First, you try to talk the problems out and negotiate a solution that leaves neither the parents nor the child feeling like a loser. Each side should give a little, compromise a little. If this is not successful, you can ask for professional counseling.

If you adopted through a nearby agency, the agency should have provided regular visits from a social worker to ensure that any problems are worked through. If your worker seems to be brushing aside your concerns, speak to her directly about this. If the problem still is ignored, ask the director of the agency for help. After the adoption is finalized, you can still go back for help.

If you are not or did not work through an agency, any nearby adoption agency should be willing to have one of their staff social workers act as family counselor. You can also call the nearest adoptive parents group (see p. 28) and ask them to recommend a family counselor with adoption experience. If these sources are not available to you, your local community mental health association or your pediatrician can recommend a counselor.

Most counselors are trained to be welcoming and impartial. If you begin to work with one with whom you feel uncomfortable, or who seems to take unfair sides or who seems to have a negative view of adoption, speak up. If it persists, consider switching. Be sure all possible causes of the problems are considered; the diagnosis and any solutions should feel "right" to all parties concerned.

Infant adoptions like older child adoptions can fail to work if temperaments clash. Babies can have physical or emotional reactions that make adjustment difficult.

Older children may be acting hostile, rejecting, overactive or passive merely because they fear rejection. Adults can have hidden motives too. The important thing is to try and uncover disrupting motives, feelings and behaviors so that they can be changed.

If your adoption has not been finalized, you have the option of not completing it. Adoption workers use the term "disruption" when a child decides to leave the family or the parents decide they want him to leave instead of making him legally their own. This is a very serious step. It can be damaging to the child and it may leave the parents with a lifetime of upset feelings. Most children from disrupted adoptions find new adoptive homes. But disruptions leave scars on all involved.

Never threaten to send a child back to the agency. If you are considering such a step, drive alone to the agency, imagining yourself taking the child back. Pretend to let him go and see how you feel. Talk over such a move with a counselor before you do it.

If the adoption is finalized, you have the same options as anyone else if problems can't be resolved. You can have the child live away from the family—in boarding school or with relatives. As a last resort, you can ask your county Deparment of Social Services to place the child in foster care.

All families have some problems. Most can be resolved given time, effort, determination and goodwill. Relationships usually grow stronger and closer after problems have been worked through. The closest and healthiest kind of family is the one that learns to talk out its differences and to share and overcome its burdens.

Part IV

THE FUTURE OF ADOPTION

15

Changing the System

Adoption as a contemporary institution can be entirely vindicated by a comparison of the groups of children born illegitimate who were adopted and who were not adopted. To be born illegitimate and to be adopted is to have an advantage which is shown in social adjustment, attainment and health. The striking success of adoption as an institution is shown by the marked extent to which adopted children mirror their not-adopted social class peers rather than the group of illegitimate children from whom they were originally drawn.[1]

Seglow, Pringle and Wedge
Child Development Researchers

Statistics show that our society has changed considerably in the past thirty years. The illegitimacy rate—the percent of babies born to unwed mothers—has skyrocketed from 4 percent in 1950 to over 17 percent today.[2] The problem is particularly acute among teen-agers. There were 554,000 babies born to teen-agers in 1978—only 31 percent were married.[3] That year 1.3 million small children were living with teen-age mothers, half of whom were unmarried.[4]

While illegitimacy has risen, the number of babies surrendered for adoption has plummeted. In 1971, 13 percent of unmarried teen-agers who gave birth chose adoption; by 1978 that figure was only 4 percent.[5]

Of course women, even girls, should be able to raise their own babies if they are able to. The problem is that many are electing to try and raise babies with little idea about the emotional responsibilities of parenting and many cannot meet the financial responsibilities. Half of the billions spent on Aid to Families with Dependent Children (the most common form of welfare) goes to families in which the woman gave birth as a teen-ager.[6] Teen-age mothers complete less schooling, tend to have larger families and, therefore, find it harder to become self-supporting.[7] They often commit themselves and their children to a life-time of poverty with little understanding of the consequences or alternatives.

It is time that our society acknowledges that parenting is an enormous responsibility. Being a parent, even with the support of a spouse and an adequate income, is a great challenge. To provide a stable and nurturing home with little education, little money and no husband requires even more maturity and skill.

More and more parents are unable to withstand the pressures of trying to raise a child under difficult circumstances, and thus, the foster care system is growing. In 1961, there were 175,000 in foster care; by 1977, there were 502,000.[8] It is estimated that a disproportionate number of these children, 47 percent, were born out of wedlock.[9]

New laws, such as the Adoption Assistance and Child Welfare Act of 1980 (federal Public Law 96–272), mandate needed reforms for adoption and foster care, but these reforms may never be adequately funded or enforced. As one researcher wrote, "The bureaucratic system has become unresponsive to the children it was designed to protect . . . [there is] a lack of leadership, conflicting policies, and regulations."[10]

The system fails too many. It often fails the very people it was designed to protect: the children and birth mothers who are frequently not beyond childhood themselves. Most of the parents and the people employed by the child welfare system usually mean well, but the system has many victims.

When Ann was just sixteen, she fell in love with Don. She knew she had found the man she would marry, so when he pressed for sex, she agreed. She thought birth control would spoil the spontaneity, and besides, she heard that if she didn't climax, she couldn't get pregnant.

Several months later, she was expecting. Her friends were excited about the news. They thought it would be wonderful to have a baby—someone all your own to love. Don was really proud, but said he was too young to get married. A teacher suggested adoption, but Ann and her friends agreed a mother would have to be unnatural to give away a baby. Ann avoided the teacher. She was planning to drop out of school anyway.

Even government officials who see the rise in teen-age pregnancy as a problem often do not think of adoption as a possible, much less positive, option. Adoption is relatively ignored by unwed mothers and those who counsel them.

For example, the Department of Social Services in New York prepared a report on teen-age pregnancy for Governor Hugh Carey.[11] The report listed the problems associated with teen-age child-rearing: the health risks to mother and child, the fact that 80 percent of girls who become mothers at seventeen or below do not complete high school, the high probability of welfare and foster care use, and the higher incidence of abuse and neglect. The report mentioned many possible government funded programs to help—education, day care, public assistance, maternity shelters. There was no program specifically designed to offer the benefits of adoption. In fact, the word "adoption" appeared only one time in the thirty pages of text and not once in the twenty-six pages of statistics.

Similarly, a Texas man in charge of a teen-age pregnancy counseling program was interviewed. He told of the many unwed girls he saw, some as young as thirteen. Of the ones giving birth, 95 percent planned to raise their babies. Most were planning to support themselves with welfare or to place the babies in government supported day care while they took CETA jobs. "These girls really want what is best for their babies," he said. The interviewer asked, "Then how can they choose to raise the babies alone and in poverty when they could be adopted by parents who could provide a stable home plus educational and financial benefits?"

The man seemed stunned by the question; he had not looked at that view. He replied, "The girls are immature. They think their child will solve their love problems. They can't get past that." Perhaps not, and they should not be forced into adoption as they were in the old days, but at least counselors should be presenting the fact that adoption could provide benefits for the child that young unwed mothers cannot.

The law will not let these young women sign a contract because they are too young to be held accountable for their decisions. We could sue the person who impregnated them for statutory rape, but our government supported programs are allowing—some say encouraging—these young women to take on the most awesome responsibility of life—the rearing of a child—without educating them to the realities of that choice.

Ann's mother was tired of raising children, but reluctantly said Ann and the baby could live with her. She warned that she was not going to baby-sit; she had a new job and a new boyfriend and was rarely home. Ann's father had moved out of town long ago.

Ann talked to a Department of Social Services' caseworker who asked if she wanted to see an adoption counselor, but dropped the subject when Ann said no. She sensed that Ann was too young and unrealistic to be a parent, but what could she do?

How to respect the rights of unwed teen-agers while letting them know the enormity of the task they are thinking of assuming? How to help them make realistic decisions during pregnancy? How to help women who bear children, but are not ready for motherhood choose adoption? One way is to present a woman with all her options and the hard-hitting reality of each choice.

Tracy Huling, who is studying adolescent pregnancy counseling for the Center for Public Advocacy Research in New York, says that counseling programs usually don't offer all options: abortion, adoption, single parenthood or marriage. "It is difficult to find a counseling program that does not have a bias or a funding restriction," she says. Often adoption is only briefly mentioned, and sometimes only to white girls. Ms. Huling says that many counselors will not mention adoption to black or Hispanic girls because of the false belief that there are no homes for minority babies.

In fact, few agencies have any black babies waiting for homes. Agencies that have black recruiting programs or allow transracial adoptions usually have families waiting for black babies. And people are spending thousands of dollars to adopt Hispanic babies from Latin America. *Any* healthy baby listed on any adoption exchange will attract dozens of prospective applicants.

In the old days, "counseling" forced girls into adoption. Today's "counseling" produces single parents. But the end results are the same: too many women who cannot live with the choice they made. True counseling informs a client of *all* options, helps her take a realistic look at the consequences of each choice and then leaves the final decision to her.

There are many government supported programs to help women and girls who want to keep their babies. There are few programs to support those who choose adoption. Adoption can provide a fresh start and a positive future for young women and their babies—it should get equal support as single parenting. And it needs support because it is no longer an option most pregnant girls consider. There is intense peer pressure on many pregnant women based on the myth that adoption is not good for babies and mothers or that adoptive homes cannot provide the same love as biological ones. Preventive education and pregnancy counseling must acknowledge and dispel these myths. Plus, there must be support for girls choosing adoption.

Currently, many girls can only find such support through independent adoption. Adoption agencies often lobby to make independent adoptions illegal. Instead, more agencies should try to offer the same legitimate benefits as independent adoption.

Women who are pregnant often want to leave their homes or work environment to avoid pressure to keep their babies or to avoid the stigma of an illegitimate birth. They often need a place to live and financial support for living expenses and medical costs. Many of these young women recoil at becoming part of the welfare system—the only support that most agencies offer. Few agencies have the funds even to pay all medical expenses, much less some living expenses.

Other benefits of independent adoption that some, not all, birth mothers want involve some control over the future of their babies and themselves. Some want their decision to choose adoption respected; they see extensive agency counseling as discouraging them from adoption rather than helping. Some birth mothers want to be able to select some characteristics that the adoptive home will have. Often such a request is merely that the home be located near a city or in the country, or else that the child grow up in a family that loves music or some other activity that means a lot to the birth mother. Having a say about the characteristics of the adopters can give birth mothers a greater sense of peace about their choice of adoption. Finally, girls who choose adoption want a better future for themselves. Some independent adoptions offer money for future education or endeavors. This is clearly illegal and agencies should not try to match this, but what they can and should provide is vocational and educational counseling.

The Edna Gladney Home, an agency providing maternity and adoption services in Forth Worth, Texas, offers all these benefits. They provide cheerful living space and a chance for a pregnant girl to get away from the pressures of her home environment. What makes Gladney unique is its active program through which each resident makes a realistic plan for herself and her baby's future. While Gladney accepts any pregnant woman—including those who say they want to keep their babies—95 percent of the 400 women who deliver at Gladney each year choose an adoption plan for their babies. They feel comfortable about their decision and there has never been a lawsuit by a resident claiming a Gladney caseworker pressured her to surrender her baby.

Why are Gladney's results the opposite of most agencies and homes? Because their whole program is directed toward having residents make their own plan for their future, but ensuring that these plans are realistic. The director, Ruby Lee Piester, says, "If the girls think you're just after their baby, they turn off. But they realize we're out to help them and they pick up quick on this."

Girls are constantly told their choice is their own, but any plan they make comes hard up against reality. Girls wanting to be single mothers need to plan for how they will support themselves and their babies. They face the realities of budgets, expected earnings and day care. Those interested in welfare meet with a welfare counselor to find out about the income they will have to live on, and then are taken apartment hunting to actually see the neighborhoods and dwellings they can afford.

Gladney always presents adoption as a positive alternative, but it is always shown realistically. Girls meet with adoptees, parents who have adopted and other girls who have chosen adoption, so that they can dispel any negative myths they hold, plus get a realistic view of this choice. Girls are encouraged to think about the kinds of parents and homes they want for their babies, and may request any characteristic or quality they want the person who adopts their baby to have.

While Gladney allows girls to make any choice, they do not encourage single parenting. There are no child-care courses given at Gladney, only academic courses and vocational counseling. Girls electing to raise their babies are referred to parenting courses in their community. Girls are encouraged to see their babies, but are also encouraged to wait to do so until two days after the birth. This gives them perspective on their experiences.

Gladney is not for everyone. About 600 girls make contact each year and 200 decide to leave before delivery. Some of these have decided to marry, others to abort. Many others do not like the focus on realistic planning or do not want to live in a place with strict codes forbidding drinking, drugs and dating while in residence. Others from outside the area who decide to keep their babies are encouraged to go home and develop the support systems a single mother needs in advance of the birth: to test out this choice before being locked into it.

No girl leaves Gladney without a positive plan for the future. They can stay as long as they want after delivery, as long as they are under a casework plan, but as one resident said, "Girls don't want to stay around too long because of the three D's—no drugs, drinking or dating. Most girls feel good about their experience and are ready to leave." They return for a six-week postpartum checkup and can receive nonidentifying information about their baby's home and how he is adjusting.

Girls pay what they can to stay at Gladney. Adopters pay fees of not more than $5,000, although the cost to Gladney is about $8,000. The difference is made up through fund raising and donations. Gladney feels strongly that as a nonprofit, privately run agency, they can be more effective than a government run one. They are not looking for government funding, but believe that it would be in each state's best interest to contribute toward maternity home costs of young women who opt for adoption, since adoption is much cheaper for states than foster care or a life of welfare dependency. Gladney is different in that it actively offers adoption, while many other maternity homes actively train a pregnant girl to be a single parent.

Ann named her beautiful baby Donna. She loved playing with Donna and dressing her up in pretty clothes. Ann's friends dropped by often. So did Don. But after the first year, things started falling apart. Don had another girl friend and rarely came around. Friends came less; they were interested in dates and school. Ann's mother was never home, and the apartment was lonely.

Motherhood bore down on Ann. She had to get out and have some fun! So she began leaving Donna at home alone at night. Neighbors complained to officials about a baby crying in the apartment. Ann agreed to place Donna in foster care for a little while—just until she got herself together.

Funding officials should look at counseling programs to see what percent of mothers are choosing adoption vs. keeping their baby. Of those who choose adoption, how many have serious regrets about that decision? Of those who keep their child, what are the success and failure indicators for mother and child? Which programs and laws produce stable family units and which do not?

One area of the law that needs scrutiny concerns the responsibilities a state assumes when a minor's parents refuse to be responsible for either their child or grandchild. One report[12] states, "Some of the adverse consequences of early child bearing are mitigated when the teenage mother and her child get parental assistance." The report shows teen-age mothers who live at home are more likely to complete school, get jobs and avoid welfare. Plus, their child's cognitive development is superior to that of a baby raised by an unwed mother alone. The grandparents' involvement must be positive, however.

New York State, for example, has several options a minor may choose if her parents will not help, but some officials who administer the programs have serious concerns about them. Although the state is trying to limit this option, the baby can be placed in foster care until the mother "grows up" and can care for it. Alternately, mother and child can be placed together as foster children. Such foster care is very expensive and not very effective in training women for life as a single parent.[13] Sometimes a teen-ager can have herself declared an "emancipated minor" as a means of obtaining a separate Aid to Families with Dependent Children welfare grant, which provides independent living quarters away from home for mother and child. But the pressure of living alone in poverty and trying to raise a child can be disastrous. Initial studies indicate up to one quarter of all emancipated minors are referred to Child Protective Services for abuse or neglect within one year.[14] It is very expensive and not very effective when the state assumes responsibilities parents refuse to accept for their pregnant children.

The government provides foster care for children whose parents neglect, abuse or abandon them. Foster care is also available when any difficult circumstance makes it impossible for a parent to continue to have the child at home. Foster care is supposed to be a temporary shelter. It has become a way of life, and the problem is most acute with the youngest children who enter foster care.

One researcher[15] found that children who enter the foster care system under the age of two spend a mean time of 7.4 years in foster care and live in several different foster homes. Half of the children under five years of age in this study had not been visited by their parents in six months. Many didn't even know their parents' name. These young children are the most adoptable, yet they often grow up in the impermanence of foster care. Other studies in other states have almost identical findings.[16]

Children need the security and stability of permanent parents who will care about them for life. Many foster parents are kind and loving, others are not, but all are paid custodians—not real parents like biological or adoptive ones.

Children are supposed to be returned home from foster care as soon as possible. If a return is not possible, they are supposed to be freed for adoption with all possible speed. The system often simply does not work this way.

Foster care workers have been accused of keeping children in foster care because the daily payments from government pay their salary. Foster care officials contend the reason children stay so long in the impermanence of foster care is not so malicious. They say foster care workers are not trained in the benefits or methods of adoption, and are often overwhelmed by large case loads. Plus, they ask, how do you face a mother whose child is a long-term foster care resident and tell her if she can not resume care for her child you are going to ask the courts to allow the child to be adopted?

Donna went to live with a nice foster family and adjusted well. Unfortunately, they had to move out of state, but Donna did fine in another new home. She enjoyed her mother's visits. Donna's second foster family needed her room for an aging relative, and Donna began having tantrums and wetting the bed when she moved to her third foster home.

By the time she was six, Donna rarely saw her mother. Life never seemed to straighten out for Ann, but she was always sure that in just a few more months she would have a steady job and a nice place of her own. She even planned to have a pink room for Donna and to buy her a canopy bed.

The caseworker suggested that Donna come home, but Ann wasn't ready. She suggested freeing Donna for adoption, but Ann cried and said that life wasn't worth living without her baby—her child was the only thing that made her keep trying to succeed.

Sydney Duncan, director of Homes for Black Children in Detroit, says, "We have to come to terms with the fact that agencies cannot parent children. It is hard when a mother says, 'I want them, but I cannot take care of them.' Often parents can give their child to a social worker when they trust that worker to find a secure adoptive home for the child."

Ms. Duncan continues, "I don't believe in snatching other people's children, and many children can go home if services are offered to the parents." But she, like others, is calling for foster care to return to being only a temporary placement . . . while recognizing how difficult this will be.

The issues surrounding the limiting of foster care are complex and there are no simple answers. The rights of parents, children and taxpayers are often at odds, and each case has extenuating—and often heartbreaking—circumstances.

When Donna was nine, the foster care agency noticed that Ann had not visited in over a year. They decided to try and terminate Ann's parental rights and began preadoptive counseling for Donna.

Donna was living in a group home for foster children. She had seen so many friends and foster parents come and go that she rarely allowed herself to care about anyone anymore. She had little belief in any promise made to her. Occasionally, when she felt low, she would lie or steal something.

In the Adoption Assistance and Child Welfare Act of 1980, the federal government mandates that states provide plans to keep a child at home, if possible, instead of entering foster care. Once in foster care, the law requires the case be reviewed after eighteen months to determine if the child can be returned home or freed for adoption. The question is, How to fund and enforce these mandates? How to make agencies accountable for implementing these laws?

New York State passed a similar law several years ago and authorized unlimited funds for "preventive services"—homemakers, day care, alcohol treatment, counseling—to help troubled families keep their children at home instead of placing them in foster care. Few states will probably do the same in light of federal and state budget cuts, although preventive services are probably cheaper than foster care.

New York City has one of the most active programs in the country to make foster care agencies more accountable and effective. It began several years ago, when Carol Bellamy, president of the City Council, found herself approving million-dollar appropriations for foster care institutions, although there were few contractual standards set on their performance. Plus there were no methods of enforcing the planning required to assure each child of a permanent home.

She ordered the system studied and found that the criteria that in the past was assumed to indicate high-quality foster care—the number of workers per child or the cost of care per child—was unrelated to how effective an agency was in planning for permanent homes for children in their care. She also discovered that agencies were not encouraging adoptions—only half of the applicants to adopt legally free foster children were even screened in the year they applied to adopt.[16]

Ms. Bellamy was concerned about the welfare of the children plus the $6,000 per child per year on average it costs taxpayers to keep a child in foster care in New York City.[17] She ordered standards set for foster homes (for example, no foster parents can be approved if they have abuse or neglect charges on their records), for home studies (for example, no discrimination in terms of race, sex or religion; applicants must be approved or rejected within ten months of application for a photo-listed child). More important, firm standards were set to limit the time a child can stay in foster care. For example, termination of parental rights proceedings must begin if a parent fails for a year to make a plan for his child to return home, or if a parent does not have contact with a child for six months. Children must be returned to their homes within two years of entering foster care in New York City or be freed for adoption. Adoption is to take place no more than three years from entering foster care. These standards sound harsh to some, especially those who do not understand a child's need for permanent love and a stable home. Two or three years of instability is an enormous amount of time in the life of a young child.[18]

To make agencies accountable for enforcing these standards, quarterly reports are issued showing where agencies are lagging. These reports are derived from standardized forms agencies submit showing, for example, how many children have been in care for a year without a plan to return home, or how many children have been in care for two years without a plan for adoption. These forms are part of the billing system—no forms, no reimbursements. Contracts for foster care will not be renewed for agencies that continue not to meet the city's standards.

A year later, as part of her preadoptive counseling, a caseworker took Donna to a Christmas party sponsored by a local adoptive parents group. Marlene and Phil met Donna there.

Marlene and Phil had wanted a big family. They saved for a house and bought one that had a swing set in the backyard. But they never had children for those swings. They decided to adopt a year ago, but never found an agency that would even invite them in for an initial meeting, much less hold out any hope for helping them find the baby they wanted so much.

In desperation, they called the president of an adoptive parents group. She invited them to the Christmas party. Feeling very awkward, and not knowing anyone, they began talking to Donna and were drawn to her. Secretly, Marlene and Phil thought about adopting an older child for the first time.

Foster care agencies say they are reluctant to press for children to be freed for adoption for fear there will be no parents to adopt them. But the extremely effective programs that recruit adoptive homes for special needs children show that any agency with many children waiting is probably not recruiting well or is placing unreasonable barriers to adopters.

Barbara Tremitiere of Tressler-Lutheran Social Services in York, Pennsylvania, finds homes for special needs children: older children, minority children, handicapped children and sibling groups. The only requirement she makes of applicants is the ability to love and their realistic appraisal that as parents they can meet the challenge of special needs adoption. Most of her district is rural, white and conservative, but she, with one or two other social workers, placed 1,268 special needs children for adoption between 1972 and 1980, with a disruption rate of less than 5 percent.[19]

Ms. Tremitiere attributes her success to her dramatic change in home study procedures—she uses group methods and puts the adopters, not the social workers, in charge of deciding whether or not they should adopt, and of selecting the child they want. She sees the job of social workers as educating the applicants to the difficult realities of what to expect from special needs adoption and to the parenting skills that are necessary for success. If the applicant decides to adopt, the social worker will help him implement the plan he makes for himself.

Everyone who calls the agency is invited in and made welcome. As quickly as possible, they are assigned to a group to begin their home study. Ten to sixteen applicants form a group and provide support and realistic feedback for one another. The first three sessions provide an overview of the process and feature panel presentations by people who have adopted "the child who is a challenge." They tell prospective parents what it is really like, discussing everything from bed-wetting to school problems. Some applicants drop out after these sessions realizing that special needs adoption is not for them.

Six more group sessions follow and help applicants clarify their values—what they want to get from and give to their children, and whether or not their needs and expectations can be met by becoming parents. They are taught parent effectiveness and communications skills.

After the nine group meetings, the prospective parents are assigned to visit a family who has adopted a child of the type they hope to have. There is also an individual meeting with a caseworker to discuss any problems or issues that might be uncomfortable to talk about in the group. Then the applicant writes up his own adoption plan (home study) using guidelines prepared by Ms. Tremitiere. Applicants are thus in charge of their own life plans. The staff social worker merely attaches her own summary and brief recommendation.

Throughout the home study, applicants have access to all the photo-listing books of children waiting for homes around the country so that they can pick out their child. The applicants are told, "You will be in charge of how many children you will get and what kind of child you get." Ms. Tremitiere says, "It is always amazing to see how their level of acceptance expands as they actually see pictures and read about specific waiting children. It is a constant reinforcement to my firm conviction that adoptive parents should select their own children."[20]

A staff worker says, "By changing the process—letting the applicants be in charge, but giving them good preparation—we've been successful. They are 'happy customers' and they send their friends in."

Sydney Duncan, director of Homes for Black Children in Detroit, works with a different population—urban blacks. But she and Barbara Tremitiere have much in common. They both believe in the goodness of potential adopters and the adoptability of special needs children. They both believe that agencies must take care to welcome every possible applicant and to drop all unnecessary requirements that might keep a child from a home. This philosophy has made them successful.

Ms. Duncan was asked to found the agency because there was such a large number of black children waiting for adoption in Detroit. She and her staff are committed to these children and enthusiastic about finding them permanent homes.

She knew that all black communities have a long tradition of taking in needy children. She cites studies showing blacks adopt at a much higher rate than whites,[21] they just do not adopt legally or through agencies, mainly because agencies have been intimidating in the past. Her small staff made sure the agency would be welcoming. Their emphasis was on the capacity to nurture rather than traditional requirements like a bank account, home ownership or no previous divorce.

Unlike Ms. Tremitiere, however, Ms. Duncan is a firm believer in public relations, but she says, "Social workers shouldn't try to do public relations." When she started the agency in 1972 she contacted a professional public relations woman and several reporters from local papers. By running regular pictures of children and human interest stories on adoptions in every possible medium, from the radical press to in-house company publications at the Ford Motor Company, she got 700 applications in her first five months of operation.[22] She had to stop the campaign to keep from being overwhelmed by applicants.

Homes for Black Children placed almost 400 children in its first three years of operation. Currently their placement rate is far lower because other adoption agencies no longer need to refer as many children to them.[23] Once the other agencies saw it was possible to reach out to the black community, they began placing their own children. There is a waiting list for black children in Detroit now. Ms. Duncan is trying to teach other agencies around the country her methods of success.

A week after the party, Marlene and Phil were still thinking about Donna and decided to try and find out more about her. Marlene called the various foster care agencies that had sent children to the party. The person who answered the phone at the first agency said she did not think any of their workers or children had been at the party. At the second agency, Marlene was put on hold for a long time and then told in an exasperated tone, "We have over a hundred children in our care. How do you expect me to know whether we have the Donna you are looking for?" The third agency took her name and several days later called saying, "Yes, Donna is one of our children, but she may never be free for adoption. The courts take so long in cases like this, plus Donna needs a lot of counseling. Very troubled youngster, you know."

There is a financial incentive in most states for agencies to keep children in foster care rather than find adoptive homes. Foster care agencies incur large costs in preparing a child for adoption: legal fees, casework time, administrative time, testing and so forth. Adoption fees states pay to these agencies often do not reimburse them for their expenses.[24] Furthermore, agencies that effectively return children to their biological homes or place children for adoption would find themselves financially destitute unless other foster children were assigned as replacements. Foster care children should be assigned to agencies with the best track records of helping children find permanency—either by going back home or being adopted.

It is also expensive for agencies to recruit homes for special needs children. Some of the most efficient agencies like Tressler-Lutheran in York, Pennsylvania, say their costs average about $1,340 per placement. Often costs at other agencies or for children with severe handicaps run in excess of $4,000. Agencies must usually recoup these costs by charging prospective parents for home studies and placement. Many adopters are loving enough to pay up to several thousand dollars to adopt a special needs child. Tressler-Lutheran recently had a couple that paid $1,000 to adopt a blind, deaf child. But it makes little sense for states to put such financial barriers in the way of adoption—especially when it can cost a state up to $30,000 per child per year for institutionalized foster care.[25]

Several states, for example, Michigan, Tennessee and New Jersey, have state "purchase of service" provisions to reimburse agencies for their costs in placing certain state-designated "hard-to-place" children in adoptive homes. Purchase of service provisions make it financially feasible for agencies to recruit, screen and train adopters for special needs children.

One of the most successful tools for finding homes for waiting children is the photo-listing book. Pictures and descriptions of children waiting for homes fill loose-leaf notebooks, which are sent to agencies and adoptive parents groups around the country.

Caseworkers report that many prospective adopters who initially request healthy babies can radically expand the definition of the kind of child they can love merely by looking through these books. Tressler-Lutheran Social Services credits the fact that parents select their own children from these books as one of their most important factors in their low disruption rate.

Almost any healthy child listed in these books gets adopted and often dozens of applicants apply to adopt a listed child. Children with very serious handicaps have been adopted because parents saw the picture and became involved. Adopters fly across the country to bring home children they have seen in these books. Through these books a child who is hard to place in certain areas, like a Mexican-American child in Texas, easily finds a home in other areas of the country where prejudices are different.

Most states are at least working to create photo-listing systems. However, not all of the children waiting for homes will be listed in some states. There are also states like California, where only caseworkers, not prospective adopters, are allowed to see the photo-listing books. These books should be made widely available to the public through adoptive parents groups, adoption agencies and libraries—anywhere that people can become interested in adopting waiting children.

Marlene had met a man who worked for an adoption agency at the Christmas party. She called him for advice. He was shocked that none of the foster care agencies had asked Marlene and Phil to come in for a meeting. "There are over two hundred children in foster care in this county. Many are free for adoption, and it is those agencies' job to find parents," he said. "Any agency that has a live body on the phone who might want to adopt an eleven-year-old should have dragged you into their office in delight. If Donna isn't free, there are many more who are."

He offered Marlene the same service his agency offers other prospective "special needs" parents. The agency does a home study, then tries to help find an available, suitable older child. The social worker and prospective parents look through many of the photo-listing books from exchanges around the country. He was sure they could find another healthy eleven-year-old girl.

The fee for this service would be 5 percent of the applicant's income, with a maximum fee of $2,000. Marlene and Phil would have to pay the maximum.

Phil was angry, "You mean they want us to pay $2,000 to take a child off the foster care rolls—off the taxpayer's back?" Marlene was embarrassed to repeat this to the agency; she did not want to appear cheap or unloving. On the other hand, she thought the $2,000 would be better reserved for family therapy if they were going to adopt a troubled eleven-year-old.

So far we have discussed only reforms needed to help prospective adopters. What about reforms to meet the needs of those who actually are adopted? Lost in the controversy over whether or not adoption records should be open is the fact that most adoptees merely want answers to legitimate questions about why they were surrendered for adoption or about their medical or genealogical histories.[26] Children who have had their questions answered fully, openly and in age-appropriate ways seem to have less need to try to open records or search for birth parents.[27] Laws should require agencies or courts to collect nonidentifying background information and give it to parents at adoption and file it for future questions from adoptees.

One agency that tries to disseminate such information is the Family Service Center in Springfield, Illinois. They give each parent a "baby book" when they adopt. The book tells why the parents were selected for their baby. It also contains a full history of the child, the birth and the adoption. The book includes a description of the appearance, personality, life-style and talents of both birth parents, plus a medical and genealogical history of both families. The reasons for and the birth parents' feelings about placing the baby for adoption are also in the book. These information packages are signed and dated by the social worker who wrote them, to facilitate further discussion, if desired. (See Appendix F for a sample "baby book.")

If every agency or independent go-between was required to collect such information and file it with the state, there would probably be far less need for searches and meetings with birth parents. These nonidentifying files could be kept open so that birth mothers could be allowed to add information for the child, and parents could also add information so that the birth mother could check on how the child was developing, and feel more comfortable with her choice of adoption. The various parties in adoption—birth parents, adoptee and parents—could have the information they need to feel comfortable and adjusted yet retain confidentiality. While this would not answer all questions and needs, some agencies and some states are already trying to provide full background information (except identifying information) as a compromise in the open records controversy.

In conclusion, more comprehensive and compassionate help needs to be given to prospective adopters. As probably every person reading this book knows, too many agencies are rude or unhelpful. The first contact with an agency is often overly discouraging, leaving the impression that if one does not want to adopt a severely handicapped child or wait years, there is little hope for adoption.

By providing better service and information for all prospective adopters, agencies can make their own jobs easier and more efficient. Currently, more and more parents are forming their own adoption agencies, adoption advisory services and maternity homes, filling the void left by uncaring or ineffective "professionals."

Agencies should invite all callers in for an orientation session where they provide specific and realistic information about the many adoption options people have plus an overview of local conditions and resources. Agencies can provide assistance and home studies for parents contemplating all types of adoption—infant, foreign, independent and special needs—and they can be more helpful in making sure people know all their biological options. Prospective adopters seem more than willing to support such services if they are offered by agencies.

The Episcopal Social Services in Baltimore, Maryland, is one agency that has begun to go in this direction. They used to be an agency that almost exclusively worked with couples on an individual basis and placed babies. As the number of babies available for adoption declined, they were faced with the choice of expanding their horizons or discontinuing their adoption service.

Episcopal Social Services radically changed the service they provide. Many of their new techniques are based on the methods Barbara Tremitiere devised: group counseling that provides realistic information and values clarification, plus allowing applicants to be in charge of their own adoption plans and write their own home study. However, they have expanded the options presented to applicants by offering information on infant adoption, foreign adoption and special needs adoption. They help prospective parents contact adoptive parents groups that provide additional support.

Applicants at Episcopal Social Services freely decide whether to wait for one of the few healthy American babies, pursue foreign adoption or choose special needs adoption. Caseworkers are active in the help they provide, especially for special needs adopters. They will call all over the country trying to find appropriate children who are free for adoption and waiting for homes.

Susan Weigel, one of the caseworkers at Episcopal Social Services, is enthusiastic about the new methods. She notes how many prospective adopters expand the definition of the kind of child they can love. She is also impressed by the plans adopters are able to make for themselves, saying, "I have worked with over one hundred applicants, and I only had one couple make plans with which I had to disagree."

Prospective parents who would have merely been discouraged by the unavailability of American babies are now finding children to love. And the benefits provided to homeless children are even greater than those experienced by the parents. In the future, hopefully more agencies will adopt these methods and expand them to include information on independent adoptions and biological options.

Marlene never called the agency back for a home study. Maybe she will one day. Donna's case is due to come before the courts soon, but court delays are notorious. Ann has a new boyfriend she really loves and wants to marry. She has been thinking lately that perhaps it would be better for everyone if Donna is adopted.

When the adoption system fails, there are usually no villains, only victims. We can ensure that there are fewer failures—for every controversial problem surrounding adoption today, creative and effective solutions are being developed. There is a great need for these solutions to be more widely publicized and adopted.

We need reforms at every part of the adoption system. We can develop effective pregnancy counseling to ensure that adoption is presented as a positive and realistic option to those who bear children before they can assume the responsibilities of parenthood. With better pregnancy counseling and more preventive services, fewer children need enter the foster care system. Few need grow up in the impermanence of foster care if we:

1. enforce strict standards of returning children home or freeing them for adoption

2. devise methods to determine if institutions are meeting standards

3. insist on effective adoptive home recruitment

4. enforce strict regulations requiring photo-listing of *all* children waiting for adoptive homes

5. legislate a purchase of service system that reimburses the full cost of placement.

These reforms would save the government a lot of money and the children a lot of pain.

For years our social welfare programs have grown with little effort to make them accountable for their effectiveness. Times are changing and taxpayers are demanding budget cuts. Two clear dangers exist. First is that administrators faced with reduced budgets will choose to serve fewer people in need instead of finding more effective ways of serving. The second danger is that the pendulum will swing back to old repressive ways, like forcing unwed mothers into adoption, instead of stopping at a healthy midpoint that encourages realistic policies and responsible programs that respect the rights and needs of both parents and children.

Many of the most important changes in adoption have occurred because parents have stayed involved and forced the system to work better. The advances in foreign adoption and special needs adoption, for example, were largely made by parents who concentrated their efforts in these areas.

Professionals and public officials, too, have been most effective when they concentrated their efforts and knowledge in specific areas of the child welfare system. The problem that has resulted, however, is that the system is fractionalized and beset by special interest groups that are suspicious of one another. All too often those with a special interest in baby adoption feel a bit put down by special needs adopters, who may resent foreign adoption advocates, who often have negative feelings about independent adopters. It is time to break this circle of suspicion and see that what benefits one form of adoption need not detract from another.

Officials, professionals and interested parents must coordinate their efforts. The experts in baby adoptions, special needs adoption, foster care, foreign adoption, public sector child welfare and private sector child welfare must recognize that their interests are more alike than diverse and that one segment of the child welfare system impacts on the other.

We can develop a system that offers prospective adopters more assistance and support, a system that helps birth parents make sound decisions, a system that gives adoptees enough genealogical information to avoid identity crises.

We can show that with good recruiting, there is no need for any child to be without a home. With better programs fewer children need grow up in homes where they are uncared for or unloved. No child should have to grow up in an institution or on the streets instead of a real home.

The reforms that are needed are in the best interest of all who care about adoption and child welfare. They are in the best interest of the birth mothers, the parents, the agencies, the public—and most important, the children.

Appendices

APPENDIX A

Adoption Agency in Each State

Alabama

Division of Adoptions
Dept. of Pensions and Security
64 N. Union Street
Montgomery, AL 36130
(205) 832-6150

Alaska

Adoptions
Division of Social Services
Dept of Health and Social Service
Alaska Office Bldg. Rm. 204
Ponch H-01
Juneau, AK 99811
(907) 465-3170

Arizona

Adoption Specialist
Dept. of Economic Security
1717 W. Jefferson Street
P.O. Box 6123
Phoenix, AZ 85005

Arkansas

Adoption Services
Division of Social Services
Blue Cross—Blue Shield Bldg.
7th and Gaines Street
P.O. Box 1437
Little Rock, AR 72203
(501) 371-2074

California

Adoptions Branch
Dept. of Social Services
744 P Street
Sacramento, CA 95814
(916) 445-3146

Colorado

Adoptions
Dept. of Social Services
1575 Sherman Street
Denver, CO 80203
(303) 839-2731

Connecticut

Adoption Unit
Division of Children's and Protective Services
Dept of Children and Youth Services
345 Main Street
Hartford, CT 06115
(203) 566-2387

Delaware

Adoption Coordinator
Division of Social Service
P.O. Box 309
Wilmington, DE 19899

District of Columbia

Adoptions
Bureau of Family Services
Social Rehabilitation Admin.
122 C Street, NW, Room 800
Washington, DC 20001
(202) 727-3161

Florida

Adoptions
Family and Children's Services
Social and Economic Services
Dept. of Health and
Rehabilitative Services
1321 Winewood Boulevard
Tallahassee, FL 32301
(904) 487-2383

Georgia

State Adoption Placement Unit
618 Ponce deLeon Avenue NE
Atlanta, GA 30308
(404) 894-4452

Hawaii

Family and Children's Services
Public Welfare Division
Dept. of Social Services
P.O. Box 339
Honolulu, HI 96809
(808) 548-5846

Idaho

State Adoption Coordinator
Dept. of Health and Welfare
State House
Boise, ID 83720
(208) 334-4085

Illinois

Office of Adoptions
Dept. of Children and Family
Services
510 N. Dearborn, Suite 400
Chicago, IL 60610
(312) 793-7319

Indiana

Adoptions
Division of Child Welfare
Social Services
Dept. of Public Welfare
100 N. Senate Avenue, Rm. 701
Indianapolis, IN 46204
(317) 232-4436

Iowa

Adoptions and Foster Care
Bureau of Children's Service
Division of Community Programs
Dept. of Social Services
Hoover State Office Bldg.
Des Moines, IA 50319
(515) 281-5583

Kansas

Adoption Specialist
Children and Family Service
Dept. of Social Rehabilitation
Services
Division of Children and Youth
2700 W. 6th Street
Topeka, KS 66606
(913) 296-4652

Kentucky

Adoption
Bureau of Social Services
Dept. of Human Resources
275 E. Main Street #6 West
Frankfort, KY 40621
(502) 564-6746

Louisiana

Adoptions
Division of Evaluation and Services
Dept. of Health and Human Resources
Office of Human Development
P.O. Box 44371
Baton Rouge, LA 70804
(504) 342-4029

Maine

Substitute Care
Bureau of Resource Development
Dept. of Human Services
State House
Augusta, ME 04333
(207) 289-2971

Maryland

Adoption Program Manager
Social Services Admin.
11 South Street
Baltimore, MD 21202
(301) 383-3604

Massachusetts

Adoption
Office of Social Services
Dept. of Public Welfare
600 Washington Street
Boston, MA 02111
(617) 727-6175

Michigan

Adoption
Office of Children and Youth Services
Dept. of Social Services
300 S. Capital Avenue
P.O. Box 30037
Lansing, MI 48909
(517) 373-3513

Minnesota

Adoption Unit
Department of Public Welfare
Centennial Office Bldg., 4th Fl.
Saint Paul, MN 55103
(612) 296-3740

Mississippi

Adoption
Division of Social Services
Dept. of Public Welfare
Fondren Station, P.O. Box 4321
Jackson, MS 39216
(601) 956-6725

Missouri

Public Adoption Information Service
Division of Family Services
Dept. of Social Services
Broadway State Office Bldg.
Jefferson City, MO 65101
(314) 751-2416

Montana

Community Services Division
Dept. of Social and Rehabilitation Services
P.O. Box 4210
Helena, MT 59601
(406) 449-3865

Nebraska

Foster Care and Adoption
Division of Social Services
Dept. of Public Welfare
301 Centennial Mall South 5th Fl.
P.O. Box 95026
Lincoln, NE 68509
(402) 471-3121, Ext. 210

Nevada

Protective Services and Adoption
Welfare Division
251 Jeanell Drive
Carson City, NV 89710
(702) 885-4771

New Hampshire

Adoption
Bureau of Child and Family Services
Dept. of Health and Welfare
Hazen Drive
Concord, NH 03301
(603) 271-4399

New Jersey

Adoption Unit
Division of Youth and Family Services
P.O. Box 510
Trenton, NJ 08625
(609) 292-0867

New Mexico

Adoption
Social Services Division
Dept. of Human Services
P.O. Box 2348
Santa Fe, NM 87503
(505) 827-2285

New York

Bureau of Children and Family Services
Adoption Section
Two World Trade Center Rm. 3580
New York, NY 10047
(212) 488-5290

North Carolina

Adoptions Unit
Family Services Section
Dept. of Human Resources
325 N. Salisbury Street
Raleigh, NC 27611
(919) 733-3801

North Dakota

Adoptions
Community Services
Social Service Board of North Dakota
State Capitol
Bismarck, ND 58505
(701) 224-2316

Ohio

Bureau of Children's Services
Division of Social Services
Dept. of Public Welfare
30 E. Broad Street
Columbus, OH 43215
(614) 466-2208

Oklahoma

Adoption
Division of Child Welfare
Dept. of Institutions, Social and Rehabilitative Services
P.O. Box 25352
Oklahoma City, OK 73125
(405) 521-2475

Oregon

Adoptions Unit
Children's Services Division
Dept. of Human Resources
198 Commercial Street SE
Salem, OR 97310
(503) 378-4452

Pennsylvania

Adoption
Bureau of State Supervised Programs
Office of Social Services
Dept. of Public Welfare
P.O. Box 2675
Harrisburg, PA 17120
(717) 487-4882

Rhode Island

Adoption
Child Welfare Services
610 Mount Pleasant Avenue
Providence, RI 02908
(401) 277-3945 Ext. 3470

South Carolina

Adoption Unit
Children and Family Services Division
Dept. of Social Services
P.O. Box 1520
Columbia, SC 29202
(803) 758-3905

South Dakota

Adoption
Division of Human Development
Dept. of Social Services
State Office Bldg., Illinois Street
Pierre, SD 57501
(605) 773-3227

Tennessee

Adoption
Social Services
Dept. of Human Services
410 State Office Bldg.
Nashville, TN 37219
(615) 741-1666

Texas

Adoption
Protective Services for Children Division
Dept. of Human Resources
John H. Reagan Bldg.
Austin, TX 78701
(512) 835-0440

Utah

Adoption
Children, Youth and Families
Dept. of Social Services, Suite 370
150 W. North Temple Street
Salt Lake City, UT 84103
(801) 533-7123

Vermont

Adoption Section
Dept. of Social and Rehabilitation Services
Agency of Human Services
State Office Bldg.
Montpelier, VT 05602
(802) 241-2150

Virginia

Adoption Section
Dept. of Welfare
8007 Discovery Drive
Richmond, VA 23288
(804) 281-9140

Washington

Adoptions
Bureau of Children's Services
Dept. of Social and Health Services
State Office Bldg. 2
Olympia, WA 985045
(206) 753-2178

West Virginia

Adoption
Services to Families and Children
Division of Social Services
Dept. of Welfare
1900 Washington Street
East Charleston, WV 25305
(304) 348-7980

Wisconsin

Adoption
Bureau of Children, Youth and Families
Dept. of Health and Social Services
State Office Bldg.
1 West Wilson Street
Madison, WI 53702
(608) 266-3036

Wyoming

Adoption
Dept. of Social Services
Hathaway Bldg.
Cheyenne, WY 82002
(307) 777-7561

SOURCE: Adapted from *Help in America*, Washington, DC: North American Council on Adoptable Children, 1980.

Canada:

Each province and territory has an adoption coordinator in the department responsible for child welfare services. This coordinator can tell you about the adoption laws and conditions, which vary by province. If you are unable to contact your local coordinator, the coordinator for all of Canada can help you. Contact:

Adoption Desk
Department of Health and Welfare
Brooke Claxton Building
Tunney's Pastures, Ottawa K1A 1B5
(613) 593-5818

Almost all adoption agencies in Canada are sponsored by the government. Private licensed agencies are found only in Ontario. Independent adoption is legal everywhere except Newfoundland (where it is illegal) and Ontario, (where it is legal only through private licensed sources).

APPENDIX B

State-by-State Facts

	Alabama	Alaska	Arizona
1. Average wait for a healthy white baby at a public agency	‡	3–5 years	‡
2. Average wait for a healthy white baby at a private agency	‡	3–5 years	1–2 years
3. Average wait for a healthy black baby	‡	1 year	6 months–1 year
4. Are healthy toddlers and preschoolers available?	‡	yes	yes
5. Is independent adoption legal?	yes	yes	yes
6. Can a go-between maintain confidentiality in an independent adoption?	no	yes	yes
7. Is it legal for a prospective adopter to advertise for a baby?	no	‡	yes
8. Court in charge of adoption	circuit or district	check with courts	superior
9. The length of time given a birth mother to revoke her consent*	10–42 days	10 days	none
10. Length of time between filing the petition to adopt and final adoption order	6 months	‡	6 months
11. Are sealed records available to adoptees at age 18?	partial †	no	no
12. Is there a photo-listing book of special needs children?	yes	yes	yes

* unless fraud, coercion or illegibility is proven

† records available under certain circumstances (Under court order birth certificates can be obtained in all states.)

‡ state did not supply information

Arkansas	California	Colorado	Connecticut	Delaware
‡	5–7 years	up to 2–3 years	‡	‡
‡	‡	‡	‡	‡
not long	‡	1 month	6–9 months	‡
only over four years old	‡	no	yes	‡
yes	yes	yes	no	no
yes	no	no	no	no
yes	no	yes	no	no
chancery	superior	district or juvenile	probate	family
10–30 days	until adoption is final	none	20–30 days	30 days
6 months	up to 6 months	6 months	3 months	‡
no	no	no	partial†	no
yes	yes	yes	yes	no

(This information was compiled with the cooperation of each state.)

	District of Columbia	Florida	Georgia
1. Average wait for a healthy white baby at a public agency	‡	‡	3 years
2. Average wait for a healthy white baby at a private agency	‡	up to 2 years	‡
3. Average wait for a healthy black baby	6 months	3 months	none
4. Are healthy toddlers and preschoolers available?	no	yes	no
5. Is independent adoption legal?	yes	yes	yes
6. Can a go-between maintain confidentiality in an independent adoption?	no	no	‡
7. Is it legal for a prospective adopter to advertise for a baby?	‡	yes	yes
8. Court in charge of adoption	family	circuit	superior
9. The length of time given a birth mother to revoke her consent*	‡	90 days	10 days
10. Length of time between filing the petition to adopt and final adoption order	3–4 months	3 months	2 months
11. Are sealed records available to adoptees at age 18?	no	no	no
12. Is there a photo-listing book of special needs children?	yes	yes	yes

* unless fraud, coercion or illegibility is proven

† records available under certain circumstances (Under court order birth certificates can be obtained in all states.)

‡ state did not supply information

Hawaii	Idaho	Illinois	Indiana	Iowa
‡	3 years	2–6 years	‡	6 years
‡	2 years	2–6 years	‡	2–6 years
‡	3 months	none	‡	3–4 months
yes	yes	yes	‡	no
yes	yes	yes	‡	yes
yes	yes	yes	‡	yes
yes	‡	no	‡	yes
family	magistrate	circuit	‡	district
none	30 days	none	‡	96 hours
6 months	1 month	6 months	‡	6 weeks–2 months
no	no	no	‡	no
no	no	yes	‡	no

	Kansas	Kentucky	Louisiana
1. Average wait for a healthy white baby at a public agency	‡	3–5 years	‡
2. Average wait for a healthy white baby at a private agency	1 year	3–5 years	‡
3. Average wait for a healthy black baby	up to 6 months	6 months–1 year	‡
4. Are healthy toddlers and preschoolers available?	yes	‡	yes
5. Is independent adoption legal?	yes	yes	yes
6. Can a go-between maintain confidentiality in an independent adoption?	no	yes	yes
7. Is it legal for a prospective adopter to advertise for a baby?	yes	no	yes
8. Court in charge of adoption	juvenile	circuit	district
9. The length of time given a birth mother to revoke her consent*	varies	up to 1 month	up to 30 days
10. Length of time between filing the petition to adopt and final adoption order	2–3 months	up to 3 months	6 months–1 year
11. Are sealed records available to adoptees at age 18?	yes	no	no
12. Is there a photo-listing book of special needs children?	no	yes	no

* unless fraud, coercion or illegibility is proven

† records available under certain circumstances (Under court order birth certificates can be obtained in all states.)

‡ state did not supply information

Maine	Maryland	Massachusetts	Michigan	Minnesota
1–5 years	2–5 years	‡	3–5 years	up to 5 years
1–5 years	minimum of 6 months	3–7 years	‡	up to 5 years
‡	6 months	‡	‡	‡
yes	yes	yes	‡	yes
yes	yes	no	no	no
no	no	‡	‡	‡
yes	yes	no	no	no
probate	circuit	probate	probate	juvenile or family
none	‡	none	‡	2 weeks
45 days	2 weeks–4 months	6 months	‡	3 months
no	no	no	no	partial †
yes	yes	yes	yes	yes

	Mississippi	Missouri	Montana
1. Average wait for a healthy white baby at a public agency	5–6 years	3 months–5 years	up to 2 years
2. Average wait for a healthy white baby at a private agency	‡	3 months–5 years	1–2 years
3. Average wait for a healthy black baby	6 months–1 year	3 months	6 months–1 year
4. Are healthy toddlers and preschoolers available?	yes	yes	yes
5. Is independent adoption legal?	yes	yes	yes
6. Can a go-between maintain confidentiality in an independent adoption?	‡	yes	no
7. Is it legal for a prospective adopter to advertise for a baby?	‡	‡	yes
8. Court in charge of adoption	chancery	circuit	district
9. The length of time given a birth mother to revoke her consent*	‡	1 month	none
10. Length of time between filing the petition to adopt and final adoption order	6 months	9 months	‡
11. Are sealed records available to adoptees at age 18?	no	no	no
12. Is there a photo-listing book of special needs children?	yes	yes	no

* unless fraud, coercion or illegibility is proven

† records available under certain circumstances (Under court order birth certificates can be obtained in all states.)

‡ state did not supply information

Nebraska	Nevada	New Hampshire	New Jersey	New Mexico
3–4 years	3 years	2–3 years	4–5 years	2–3 years
3–4 years	1–2 years	‡	4–5 years	2–3 years
less than 3 years	up to 6 months	‡	6 months	none
yes	yes	yes	‡	yes
yes	yes	yes	yes	yes
yes	no	yes	no	yes
yes	no	yes	yes	no
county	district	probate	county	district
none	none	none	none	none
6 months	6 months	6 months	6 months	6 months
no	no	no	no	no
no	no	no	yes	yes

	New York	North Carolina	North Dakota
1. Average wait for a healthy white baby at a public agency	1–3 years	3–4 years	3–4 years
2. Average wait for a healthy white baby at a private agency	‡	1–2 years	3–4 years
3. Average wait for a healthy black baby	‡	6–9 months	‡
4. Are healthy toddlers and preschoolers available?	‡	yes	yes
5. Is independent adoption legal?	yes	yes	no
6. Can a go-between maintain confidentiality in an independent adoption?	yes	no	no
7. Is it legal for a prospective adopter to advertise for a baby?	yes	no	‡
8. Court in charge of adoption	surrogate or family	superior	district
9. The length of time given a birth mother to revoke her consent*	1 month	1–6 months	10 days–1 month
10. Length of time between filing the petition to adopt and final adoption order	‡	1 year	20 days
11. Are sealed records available to adoptees at age 18?	no	no	partial
12. Is there a photo-listing book of special needs children?	yes	yes	no

* unless fraud, coercion or illegibility is proven

† records available under certain circumstances (Under court order birth certificates can be obtained in all states.)

‡ state did not supply information

Ohio	Oklahoma	Oregon	Pennsylvania	Rhode Island
‡	2–2½ years	1 year	5–7 years	‡
‡	2–2½ years	1 year	5–7 years	at least 1½ years
none	‡	6 months	‡	‡
‡	‡	yes	yes	yes
yes	yes	yes	yes	yes
yes	yes	yes	yes	no
no	yes	yes	yes	yes
probate	district	circuit	common pleas	family
—	1 month	varies	‡	‡
6 months	6 months	2 months	6 months	6–8 weeks
no	no	no	no	no
yes	no	no	yes	no

	South Carolina	South Dakota	Tennessee
1. Average wait for a healthy white baby at a public agency	2–4 years	‡	2–3 years
2. Average wait for a healthy white baby at a private agency	‡	‡	2 or more years
3. Average wait for a healthy black baby	1 month–1½ years	‡	2 months–1 year
4. Are healthy toddlers and preschoolers available?	yes	‡	yes
5. Is independent adoption legal?	yes	‡	yes
6. Can a go-between maintain confidentiality in an independent adoption?	yes	‡	no
7. Is it legal for a prospective adopter to advertise for a baby?	yes	‡	no
8. Court in charge of adoption	family	‡	chancery and circuit
9. The length of time given a birth mother to revoke her consent*	‡	‡	1–3 months
10. Length of time between filing the petition to adopt and final adoption order	up to 6 months	‡	6 months
11. Are sealed records available to adoptees at age 18?	no	‡	no
12. Is there a photo-listing book of special needs children?	yes	‡	yes

* unless fraud, coercion or illegibility is proven

† records available under certain circumstances (Under court order birth certificates can be obtained in all states.)

‡ state did not supply information

Texas	Utah	Vermont	Virginia	Washington
‡	2–4 years	3 years	2–5 years	‡
3–5 years	2–4 years	3 years	3–5 years	‡
6 months	‡	‡	3 months–1 year	‡
yes	yes	no	yes	‡
yes	yes	yes	yes	yes
yes	yes	yes	no	yes
yes	yes	yes	no	yes
district	district	probate	circuit	superior
‡	‡	none	none	none
‡	6 months	6 months	3 months–1 year	‡
no	no	no	yes	no
yes	yes	yes	yes	yes

	West Virginia	Wisconsin	Wyoming
1. Average wait for a healthy white baby at a public agency	‡	2 or more years	1–2 years
2. Average wait for a healthy white baby at a private agency	‡	2 or more years	1–2 years
3. Average wait for a healthy black baby	‡	up to 9 months	‡
4. Are healthy toddlers and preschoolers available?	‡	yes	‡
5. Is independent adoption legal?	‡	yes	yes
6. Can a go-between maintain confidentiality in an independent adoption?	‡	no	yes
7. Is it legal for a prospective adopter to advertise for a baby?	‡	no	no
8. Court in charge of adoption	‡	circuit	district
9. The length of time given a birth mother to revoke her consent*	‡	none	none
10. Length of time between filing the petition to adopt and final adoption order	‡	3 days	6 months
11. Are sealed records available to adoptees at age 18?	‡	no	no
12. Is there a photo-listing book of special needs children?	‡	yes	yes

* unless fraud, coercion or illegibility is proven

† records available under certain circumstances (Under court order birth certificates can be obtained in all states.)

‡ state did not supply information

APPENDIX C

Family Builders Agencies

Children Unlimited, Inc.
P.O. Box 11463
Columbia, SC 29211
(803) 799-8311

Family Builders by Adoption
Children's Home Society
3200 Telegraph Avenue
Oakland, CA 94609
(415) 654-5211

Family Builders by Adoption, Inc.
4911 Lowell Boulevard
Denver, CO 80221
(303) 455-9579

Medina Children's Service-TASC
123 6th Avenue
Seattle, WA 98122
(206) 324-9470

New York Spaulding for Children
19 W. 44th Street
New York, NY 10036
(212) 869-8940

Peirce-Warwick Adoption Service
5229 Connecticut Avenue, NW
Washington, DC 20015
(202) 966-2531

Project CAN, Family
Counseling Center
2960 Roosevelt Boulevard
Clearwater, FL 33520
(813) 531-0481

Spaulding for Children
3660 Waltrous Road
Chelsea, MI 48118
(313) 475-8693

Spaulding for Children
36 Prospect Street
Westfield, NJ 07090
(201) 233-2282

Spaulding for Children
Beech Brook
3737 Lander Road
Cleveland, OH 44124
(216) 464-4445

Spaulding Midwest
1855 N. Hillside
Wichita, KS 67214
(316) 686-6645

Spaulding Southwest
3605 N. MacGregor Way
Houston, TX 77004
(713) 522-8683

APPENDIX D

Regional Adoption Exchanges

AASK
(Aid to Adoption of Special Kids)
3530 Grand Avenue
Oakland, CA 94610
(415) 451-1748

CAP BOOK
(Council of Adoptive Parents)
33 S. Washington Street
Rochester, NY 14608
(716) 232-5110

CARE
(Children's Adoption Resource Exchange)
1039 Evarts Street, NE
Washington, DC 20017
(202) 526-5200

CHILD CARE ASSOCIATION OF ILLINOIS
Adoption Listing Service of Illinois
749 S. Grand Avenue West
Springfield, IL 62704
(217) 528-4409

DARE
(Delaware Valley Adoption Resource Exchange)
1218 Chestnut Street
Suite 204
Philadelphia, PA 19107
(215) 925-0200

NARE
(National Adoption Resource Exchange)
67 Irving Place
New York, NY 10003
(212) 254-7410

NORTHWEST ADOPTION EXCHANGE
157 Yesler Way
Suite 208
Seattle, WA 98104
(206) 623-9224

ROCKY MOUNTAIN ADOPTION EXCHANGE
7100 W. 44th
Suite 208
Wheatridge, CO 80033
(303) 471-5924

SUMA
Services to Unmarried Mothers and Adoption
1216 E. McMillan
Cincinnati, OH 45206
(513) 221-7862

TRAC
Three Rivers Adoption Council
220 Grant Street
Pittsburgh, PA 15219
(412) 261-3460

APPENDIX E

Agencies for Foreign Adoptions (U.S.A. and Canada)

U.S.A.

Americans for International
Aid and Adoption
947 Dowling Road
Bloomfield Hills, MI 48013

Children's Home Society of
Minnesota
2230 Como Avenue
St. Paul, MN 55108

Crossroads
4901 W. 77th Street
Minneapolis, MN 55435

Dillon Family and Youth
Services
2525 E. 21st Street
Tulsa, OK 74114

Friends of Children of
Viet Nam
600 Gilpin Street
Denver, CO 80218

Holt Adoption Program, Inc.
P.O. Box 2440
Eugene, OR 97402

Love the Children
221 W. Broad Street
Quakertown, PA 18951

Welcome House
P.O. Box 836
Doylestown, PA 18901

CANADA

Those interested in foreign adoption can obtain a home study through their local agency. The adoption coordinator in each province can provide a referral to a local agency. The International Adoption Coordinator in Ottawa reports that most foreign Canadian adoptees come from Korea, the Phillipines, and Hong Kong. To a lesser degree, Canadians are adopting children from Honduras, Haiti, Guatamala, India, and Bangladesh.

International Adoption
Coordinator
Department of Health and
Welfare
Brooke Claxton Building
Tunney's Pastures, Ottawa K1A 1B5

APPENDIX F

A Sample "Baby Book" of Genealogical Information

FAMILY SERVICE CENTER
of Cross County

April 15, 1982

Mr. and Mrs. Peter K. Murray
130 Wendella Avenue
Springfield, Texas 77704

Dear Mr. and Mrs. Murray:

We are presenting you with the enclosed information about your daughter for you to keep as a record of her life and background before she became a member of your family.

We hope it will remind you through the years of the happiness of your getting together. It will also serve to let your daughter know of her biological background when she wishes more information.

Once again, we wish to express our appreciation for the confidence you have shown in this agency by bringing to us your deepest needs and desires for a child. We are pleased to share in your feelings of fulfillment and happiness.

Sincerely yours,

Barry L. Leeds

LLL:vs
Enclosures

1503 SOUTHFORK STREET • TRURO, TEXAS 77777 • (713) 234-5678

FAMILY SERVICE CENTER of Cross County

FAMILY BACKGROUND AND DEVELOPMENTAL HISTORY

Heather Suzanne, your daughter, was born on March 2, 1982, in Springfield, Texas. Her delivery was spontaneous and normal and she was a healthy, well-developed newborn, although slightly premature. She remained in the hospital for a few days and was placed in a licensed agency foster home on March 6, 1982, where she remained until she was placed adoptively in your home on March 27, 1982. Details of her medical condition can be found on the attached medical sheet.

Due to a combination of important circumstances, Heather's mother felt that adoptive placement was the best plan for her and she asked the agency to find a home where Heather could be provided with love, security, and the kind of environment that would help her to develop to the best of her potentials.

The biological father also felt that the best plan for their child would be a stable, secure adoptive home. He cooperated with the mother and the agency in working out this plan.

The agency carefully followed the requirements of the laws of the State of Texas in obtaining the legal authority to place Heather for adoption. Your home was selected as the best possible placement for Heather and accordingly you saw one another for the first time on March 26, 1982. Upon your whole-hearted acceptance of her and your commitment to be her parents forever, she was placed adoptively in your home on March 27, 1982.

Heather's first mother was an attractive, nineteen-year-old young lady of French-Indian ancestry. She was five feet, six inches tall, weighed 120 pounds, had dark brown hair, blue eyes, and a medium bone structure and a medium complexion. Her health was good. She had an outgoing personality and many friends. At the time of Heather's birth, she was enrolled in her first year of college, making average to above average grades. The mother is interested in interior design and hopes to persue her career in this field. She is talented in music, having played the piano for a number of years. Her plan is to continue her college education.

The first mother's family was aware of their daughter's pregnancy and plan for adoption and supportive of that plan. The mother had two younger sisters, both of whom are in good health and enrolled in school.

1503 SOUTHFORK STREET • TRURO, TEXAS 77777 • (713) 234-5678

- 2 -

Heather's first father was also nineteen years of age, a high school graduate and enrolled in a technical school, learning drafting skills. He is five feet, ten inches tall, weighs 165 pounds, has brown curly hair, green eyes, a fair complexion and medium bone structure. His nationality background is Germen and English. He is very interested in sports, especially soccer.

The father's family was not directly involved with the agency in the adoption process. The father had an older brother who was married and in good health.

The biological parents both signed surrenders freeing Heather for adoptive placement. Their hope was that she could be placed as quickly as possible into her adoptive home. The biological parents no longer were seeing each other and each planned to complete his and her educations. Each one indicated to our agency that if Heather had a strong need to try to contact them when she reaches adulthood that they would be willing to have our agency contact them to share this information. Each hoped that Heather would understand their reasons for placing her adoptively.

The family background history includes the fact that diabetes is present in the mother's background. Her paternal grandmother was a diabetic as well as this grandmother's sister. One of the mother's sisters was allergic to penicillin.

High blood pressure runs in the biological father's family with both his parents being somewhat overweight and his father experiencing high blood pressure. Otherwise, other family members are healthy and have made good social adjustments.

FAMILY SERVICE CENTER
of Cross County

HEALTH HISTORY

Heather Suzanne Murray

Birth date:	March 2, 1982
Time:	1:20 P.M.
Gestation:	Approximately eight and one half months
Delivery:	Normal, spontaneous
Birth weight:	5 pounds 12 ounces
Birth length:	18½ inches
Head Circumference:	13½ inches
Chest Circumference:	13 inches
Apgar rating:	7 at 1 minute
	9 at 5 minutes
Formula:	Enfamil with iron
Discharge:	March 6, 1982
Discharge weight:	5 pounds 10 ounces

Heather was placed in foster care on March 6, 1982, where her progress was normal. She was a good eater and quickly began to gain weight.

During a pediatric check-up on 3/20/82, Heather weighed 6 pounds 6 ounces, was taking her formula well, and sleeping well. No medical problems were noted. She is to return to the pediatrician at the age of two months to begin her immunizations.

1503 SOUTHFORK STREET • TRURO, TEXAS 77777 • (713) 234-5678

ADOPTIVE AGREEMENT

The Family Service Center of Cross County is pleased to enter into this agreement to place Heather Suzanne, born March 2, 1982 for adoption in the home of Peter and Harriet Murray, living at 130 Wendella Avenue, Springfield, Texas 77704. The parents, Mr. and Mrs. Peter Murray, agree to accept this child into their home and commit themselves to the permanent parenthood of this child, including the responsibilities of love, care, training, and the provision of food, clothing, shelter and medical care.

For the period of about one year from the time of placement, the Family Service Center of Cross County will continue to hold legal authority under the Adoption Act of the State of Texas for the permanent planning for this child. During this time, the agency will have periodic personal contacts with the parents and the child, to promote the growth of and healthy development of the parent-child relationships begun by this placement. The parents agree to make themselves, their children, and their home available for these contacts. The parents further agree that at the suggestion of the agency, they will employ an attorney (all legal fees and court costs to be paid by the adopting parents) to take the necessary legal steps to obtain a decree of adoption. The agency agrees to make necessary information and documents available to this attorney, to report on the progress of the adoption to the court hearing the parent's petition for a decree of adoption, and to execute its legal consent to a final decree of adoption of this child by these parents, unless there is sufficient cause to withhold such consent.

This agreement may be terminated prior to the legal completion of the adoption only under the following extreme circumstances: (1) when in the judgment of the agency or the parents the well-being of the parents, child to be adopted, or any other family member would be jeopardized by continuing the adoptive placement; or (2) if some condition not known at the time of the placement has developed in the child which makes him unacceptable to the parents or whose care on account of such condition would place an unreasonable burden on the parents.

Peter K. Murray — Adoptive Father

Harriet Murray — Adoptive Mother

Lisa Douglas — Executive Director

Esther Hernandez — Witness

March 27, 1982 — Date

SOURCES AND NOTES

INTRODUCTION (pages xi–xix)

Sources

Anderson, David. *Children of Special Value: Interracial Adoption in America.* New York: St. Martin's Press, 1971.

Bass, Celia. "Matchmaker-Matchmaker: Older-Child Adoption Failures." *Child Welfare,* vol. LIV, no. 7 (July 1975): 505–510.

Barbour, John. "Three Generations of Women, Three Lifestyles." *St. Petersburg Times,* June 3, 1979, pp. 1A, 12A.

Benet, Mary Kathleen. *The Politics of Adoption.* New York: The Free Press, 1976.

Bureau of the Census. *Statistical Abstract of the United States.* Washington, DC: U.S. Government Printing Office, 1980.

Cover Story: Adoption in America Transcript. Pittsburgh: PTV Publications, 1980.

"D.C. Foster Care: Wards of the Bureaucracy." *Adoptalk,* vol. 6, no. 6 (July 1981): 4.

Elonen, Anna, and Schwartz, Edward. "A Longitudinal Study of Emotional, Social and Academic Functioning of Adopted Children." *Children Welfare,* vol. XLVIII, no. 2 (February 1969): 72–78.

Fanshel, David. "Children Discharged from Foster Care." *Child Welfare,* vol. LVII, no. 8 (September/October 1978): 72–78.

———. "Preschoolers Entering Foster Care: The Need to Stress Plans for Permanency." *Child Welfare,* vol. LVIII, no. 2 (February 1979): 67–87.

Goldstein, Joseph, et al. *Beyond the Best Interests of the Child.* Glencoe, NY: The Free Press, 1973.

Grow, Lucille, and Shapiro, Deborah. *Black Children White Parents: A Study of Transracial Adoption.* New York: Child Welfare League of America, 1974.

Hoeppner, Marie. *Where Have All the Children Gone?* Santa Monica: The Rand Corporation, 1977.

Hoopes, Janet, et al. *A Follow-up of Adoptions.* New York: Child Welfare League of America, 1970.

Jaffee, Benson. "Adoption Outcome: A Two-Generational View." *Child Welfare,* vol. 53, no. 4 (April 1974): 211–224.

Jaffee, Benson, and Fanshel, David. *How They Fared in Adoption: A Follow-Up Study.* New York: Columbia University Press, 1970.

Jewett, Claudia. *Adoptalk,* vol. 5, no. 9 (October 1980): 2.

Jones, Charles, and Else, John. "Racial and Cultural Issues in Adoption." *Child Welfare,* vol. LVIII, no. 6 (June 1979): 373–382.

Kadushin, Alfred. *Adopting Older Children.* New York: Columbia University Press, 1970.

———. *Child Welfare Services.* 3d ed. New York: MacMillan, 1980.

Kadushin, Alfred, and Seidl, Frederick. "Adoption Failure: A Social Work Postmortem." *Social Work,* vol. 16 (July 1971): 32–37.

Kim, S. Peter, et al. "Adoption of Korean Children by New York Area Couples." *Child Welfare,* vol. LVIII, no. 7 (July/August 1979): 419–428.

Kirk, H. David, et al. "Are Adopted Children Especially Vulnerable to Stress?" *Archives of General Psychiatry,* vol. 14 (March 1966): 291–298.

Klibanoff, Susan, and Klibanoff, Elton. *Let's Talk About Adoption.* Boston: Little, Brown, 1973.

Kornitzer, Margaret. *Adoption and Family Life.* New York: Humanities Press, 1968.

Lifton, Betty Jean. *Twice Born: Memoirs of an Adopted Daughter.* New York: McGraw-Hill, 1975.

Luckey, Eleanore, and Baim, Joyce. "Children: A Factor in Marital Satisfaction." *Journal of Marriage and the Family* 32 (1) (1970): 43–44.

McNamara, Joan. *The Adoption Adviser.* New York: Hawthorn Books, 1975.

McWhinnie, Alexina. *Adopted Children: How They Grow Up.* London: Routledge & Kegan Paul, 1967.

Martin, Katherine. *Teenage Pregnancy: A Discussion of the Problem.* White Plains, NY: Department of Social Service, 1979.

Menning, Barbara. "The Infertile Couple: A Plea for Advocacy." *Child Welfare*, vol. LIV, no. 6 (June 1975): 454–460.

National Center for Social Statistics. *Adoptions in 1975.* Washington: U.S. Government Printing Office, 1977.

———. *Monthly Vital Statistics Report.* vol. 30, no. 6 (September 29, 1981).

North American Center on Adoption. *Adoption Notebook.* New York: Child Welfare League of America, 1978.

Philliber, Susan, and Rothenberg, Pearilla. *The Impact of Single Parenthood on Mothers and Their Children.* New York: Center for Population and Family Health, Columbia University, 1980.

Plumez, Jacqueline. "Adoption: Where Have All the Babies Gone?" *The New York Times Magazine* (April 13, 1980): 34–42, 105–106.

Raymond, Louise. *Adoption and After.* Rev. ed. New York: Harper & Row, 1974.

Seglow, Jean, et al. *Growing Up Adopted.* Windsor: National Foundation for Education and Research in England and Wales, 1972.

Shyne, Ann. "Who Are the Children? A National Overview of Services." *Social Work Research and Abstracts*, vol. 16, no. 1 (Spring 1980): 26–33.

Shyne, Ann, and Schroeder, Anita. *National Study of Social Services.* Washington: Department of Health, Education and Welfare, 1978.

Skeels, Harold. "Adult Status of Children with Contrasting Early Life Experiences: A Follow-Up Study." *Monographs of the Society for Research in Child Development*, vol. 31, no 3 (1966).

Skeels, Harold, and Harms, Irene. "Children With Inferior Social Histories; Their Mental Development in Adoptive Homes." *Journal of Genetic Psychology*, vol. 72 (1948): 283–294.

Skodak, Marie, and Skeels, Harold. "A Final Follow-Up Study of 100 Adopted Children." *Journal of Genetic Psychology*, vol. 75 (1949): 85–125.

Sorosky, Arthur, et al. *The Adoption Triangle: The Effects of the Sealed Record on Adoptees, Birth Parents and Adoptive Parents.* Garden City, NY: Anchor Press/Doubleday, 1978.

Steketee, John. "Concern for Children in Placement." *Adoption Report*, vol. 3, no. 2 (Spring 1982): 2.

Stonesifer, Elsie. "The Behavior Difference of Adopted and Own Children." *Smith College Studies of Social Work*, vol. 13 (1942): 161.

Teenage Pregnancy: A Report to Governor Hugh L. Carey. Albany: New York State Department of Social Services, 1978.

Teenage Pregnancy: The Problem That Hasn't Gone Away. New York: The Alan Guttmacher Institute, 1981.

Triseliotis, John. *In Search of Origins*. London: Routledge & Kegan Paul, 1973.

Winick, Margaret, et al. "Malnutrition and Environmental Enrichment by Adoption." *Science*, vol. 190 (1975): 1173–1175.

Witmer, Helen, et al. *Independent Adoptions: A Follow-Up Study*. New York: Russell Sage Foundation, 1963.

Zur Nieden, Margaret. "The Influence of Constitution and Environment Upon the Development of Adopted Children." *Journal of Psychology*, vol. 31 (1951): 91–95.

Notes

1. Shyne, 1980.
2. Kornitzer, 1968.
3. Kadushin and Seidl, 1971.
4. Jewett, 1980, p. 2.
5. Luckey and Baim, 1970.
6. Anderson, 1971; Grow and Shapiro, 1974; Kadushin, 1980; Kim et al., 1979; Kornitzer, 1968; Witmer et al., 1973; Zur Nieden, 1951.
7. Kadushin, 1970.
8. Elonen and Schwartz, 1969; Hoopes et al., 1970; Kirk, 1966; Stonesifer, 1942; Witmer, 1963.
9. Seglow et al., 1972.
10. Raymond, 1974.
11. Hoeppner, 1977; Philliber and Rothenberg, 1980; Seglow et al., 1972; Sorosky et al., 1978; *Teenage Pregnancy*, 1978, 1981.
12. Winick et al., 1975.
13. Skeels, 1966; Skeels and Harms, 1948; Skodak and Skeels, 1949; Zur Nieden, 1951.
14. Ibid.

15. Kadushin, 1980.
16. Bureau of the Census, 1980; National Center for Social Statistics, 1981.
17. *Teenage Pregnancy*, 1981.
18. *Teenage Pregnancy*, 1978.
19. *Teenage Pregnancy*, 1981.
20. Martin, 1979.
21. *Teenage Pregnancy*, 1981.
22. *Teenage Pregnancy*, 1978.
23. Martin, 1979.
24. *Teenage Pregnancy*, 1978.
25. "D.C. Foster Care . . . ," 1981; Fanshel, 1978, 1979; Steketee, 1978.
26. Ibid.
27. National Center for Social Statistics, 1977.
28. Menning, 1975.
29. Ibid.
30. National Center for Social Statistics, 1977.
31. North American Center on Adoption, 1978.
32. Lifton, 1975.
33. Sorosky et al., 1978.
34. Sorosky et al., 1978; Triseliotis, 1973.

PART I

1. SHOULD YOU ADOPT? (pages 1–9)

Sources

Anderson, David. *Children of Special Value: Interracial Adoption in America*. New York: St. Martin's Press, 1971.

Arnold, Fred, et al. *The Value of Children: A Cross-National Study*. vol. 1. Honolulu: East-West Population Institute, 1975.

Berman, Claire. *We Take This Child: A Candid Look at Modern Adoption*. Garden City, NY: Doubleday, 1974.

Chess, Stella. *An Introduction to Child Psychiatry*. New York: Greene and Stratton, 1969.

Eiduson, Bernice, and Livermore, Jean. "Complications in Therapy With Adopted Children." *The American Journal of Orthopsychiatry*, vol. 23 (October 1953): 795–802.

Elonen, Anna, and Schwartz, Edward. "A Longitudinal Study of Emotional, Social and Academic Functioning of Adopted Children." *Child Welfare*, vol. XLVIII, no. 2 (February 1969): 72–78.

Humphrey, Michael, and Ounstead, Christopher. "Adoptive Families Referred for Psychiatric Advice." *British Journal of Psychiatry*, vol. CIX (September 1963): 599–608.

Jaffee, Benson, and Fanshel, David. *How They Fared in Adoption: A Follow-Up Study*. New York: Columbia University Press, 1970.

Krugman, Dorothy. "Reality in Adoption." *Child Welfare* (July 1964): 349–358.

Lawder, E. A. *A Follow-Up Study of Adoption: Post Placement Functioning of Adoption Families.* New York: Child Welfare League of America, 1969.

McNamara, Joan. *The Adoption Adviser.* New York, Hawthorn Books, 1975.

McWhinnie, Alexina. *Adopted Children: How They Grow Up*. London: Routledge & Kegan Paul, 1967.

Menning, Barbara. "The Infertile Couple: A Plea for Advocacy." *Child Welfare*, vol. LIV, no. 6 (June 1975): 454–460.

Raymond, Louise. *Adoption and After.* Rev. ed. New York: Harper & Row, 1974.

Ryder, Robert. "Longitudinal Data Relating Marriage Satisfaction and Having a Child." *Journal of Marriage and the Family*, vol. 35, no. 4 (April 1973): 604–608.

Sorosky, Arthur, et al. *The Adoption Triangle: The Effect of The Sealed Record on Adoptees, Birth Parents and Adoptive Parents.* Garden City, NY: Anchor Press/Doubleday, 1978.

Triseliotis, John. *In Search of Origins.* London: Routledge & Kegan Paul, 1973.

Zur Nieden, Margaret. "The Influence of Constitution and Environment Upon the Development of Adopted Children." *Journal of Psychology* 31 (1951): 91–95.

Notes

1. Arnold, et al., 1975.
2. Ryder, 1973.
3. Menning, 1975.

4. Krugman, 1964.
5. Jaffee and Fanshel, 1970; McWhinnie, 1967; Triseliotis, 1973.
6. Eiduson and Livermore, 1953; Humphrey and Ounstead, 1963.
7. Anderson, 1971.

2. WHAT KIND OF CHILD? (pages 11–17)

Sources

Anderson, David. *Children of Special Value: Interracial Adoption in America*. New York: St. Martin's Press, 1971.

Berman, Claire. *We Take This Child: A Candid Look at Modern Adoption*. Garden City, NY: Doubleday, 1974.

Blank, Joseph. *Nineteen Steps Up the Mountain: The Story of the DeBolt Family*. New York: J. B. Lippincott, 1976.

Buck, Pearl. *Children for Adoption*. New York: Random House, 1964.

Carney, Ann. *No More Here and There: Adopting the Older Child.* Chapel Hill: University of North Carolina Press, 1976.

Child Welfare League of America Standards for Adoption Service. New York: Child Welfare League of America, 1978.

Cover Story: Adoption in America Transcript. Pittsburgh: PTV Publications, 1980.

Grow, Lucille, and Shapiro, Deborah. *Black Children White Parents: A Study of Transracial Adoption*. New York: Child Welfare League of America, 1974.

Jewett, Claudia. *Adopting the Older Child*. Harvard: The Harvard Common Press, 1978.

Kadushin, Alfred. *Child Welfare Services*. 3d ed. New York: MacMillan, 1980.

Klein, Carol. *The Single Parent Experience*. New York, Avon, 1973.

Klibanoff, Susan, and Klibanoff, Elton. *Let's Talk About Adoption*. Boston: Little, Brown, 1973.

Krugman, Dorothy. "Reality in Adoption." *Child Welfare* (July 1964): 349–358.

McNamara, Joan. *The Adoption Adviser*. New York: Hawthorn Books, 1975.

Raymond, Louise. *Adoption and After.* Rev. ed. New York: Harper & Row, 1974.

Who Are the DeBolts? (film). Mill Valley, Calif.: Korty Film, 1978.

Notes

1. Anderson, 1971; Grow and Shapiro, 1974; Kadushin, 1980.
2. Klibanoff and Klibanoff, 1973.
3. Child Welfare League, 1978.
4. Buck, 1964.
5. *Who Are the DeBolts?*, 1978.

PART II

3. ASSESSING YOUR OPTIONS (pages 21–28)

Sources

City Council President's Adoption Research Project. New York: The City of New York, 1980.

Rankin, Deborah. "Adoption Costs as a Job Benefit." *The New York Times,* November 1, 1980, p. 32.

Notes

1. *City Council President's Adoption Research Project,* 1980.
2. Ibid.

4. BIOLOGICAL OPTIONS (pages 29–35)

Sources

American Fertility Society. *How to Organize a Basic Study of the Infertile Couple.* Birmingham: The American Fertility Society, Undated.

Castillo, Angel. "When Women Bear Children for Others." *The New York Times,* December 22, 1980.

———. "Drug May Help Up to 10% of Infertile Adults." *St. Petersburg Times,* September 25, 1980, p. 1.

Fleming, Anne Taylor. "New Frontiers in Conception." *The New York Times Magazine,* July 20, 1980, pp. 14–23, 42–52.

———. "Health Focus." *Glamour Magazine*, October 1980, p. 44.

Hoeppner, Marie. *Where Have All the Children Gone? The Adoption Market Today*. Santa Monica, CA: The Rand Corporation, 1977.

Kistner, Robert. "The Infertile Woman." *American Journal of Nursing*, vol. 73, no. 11 (November 1973): 1937–1943.

Menning, Barbara. "The Infertile Couple: A Plea for Advocacy." *Child Welfare*, vol. LIV, no. 6 (June 1975): 454–460.

Quindlen, Anna. "Surrogate Mothers: A Controversial Solution to Infertility." *The New York Times*, May 27, 1980, p. B12.

Notes.

1. Hoeppner, 1977, p. 2.
2. Ibid., p. 6.
3. "Drug May Help Up to 10% of Infertile Adults," 1980.

5. AGENCY ADOPTIONS (pages 37–46)

Sources

Adoption: A Guide to Adopting in the New York Area. New York: The New York Junior League, 1980.

Berman, Claire. *We Take This Child: A Candid Look at Modern Adoption*. Garden City, NY: Doubleday, 1974.

Farmer, Robert. *How to Adopt a Child*. New York: Arco, 1967.

Listing of Licensed Adoption Agencies in the United States. New York: North American Center on Adoption, 1978.

McNamara, Joan. *The Adoption Adviser*. New York: Hawthorn Books, 1975.

Raymond, Louise. *Adoption and After*. Rev. ed. New York: Harper & Row, 1974.

Sorosky, Arthur, et al. *The Adoption Triangle*. Garden City, NY: Anchor Press/Doubleday, 1978.

6. SPECIAL NEEDS ADOPTIONS (pages 47–68)

Sources

Adopting. Albany: New York State Department of Social Services, Undated.

Anderson, David. *Children of Special Value: Interracial Adoption in America.* New York: St. Martin's Press, 1971.

Berman, Claire. *We Take This Child: A Candid Look at Modern Adoption.* Garden City, NY: Doubleday, 1974.

Blank, Joseph. *Nineteen Steps Up the Mountain: The Story of the DeBolt Family.* New York: Lippincott, 1976.

Carney, Ann. *No More Here and There: Adopting the Older Child.* Chapel Hill: University of North Carolina Press, 1976.

City Council President's Adoption Research Project. New York: The City of New York, 1980.

Flynn, Laurie. "Why Would Anyone Adopt a Teenager?" *Change,* vol. 4, no. 3 (Fall 1980): 6, 13.

Gallagher, Ursula. "The Adoption of Mentally Retarded Children." *Children,* vol. 15, no. 1 (January/February 1968): 17–21.

Goldstein, Joseph, et al. *Beyond the Best Interest of the Child.* Glencoe, NY: The Free Press, 1973.

Grow, Lucille, and Shapiro, Deborah. *Black Children White Parents: A Study of Transracial Adoption.* New York: Child Welfare League of America, 1974.

Jewett, Claudia. *Adopting the Older Child.* Harvard: Harvard Common Press, 1978.

Jones, Martha. "Preparing the School Age Child for Adoption." *Child Welfare,* vol. LVIII, no. 1 (January 1979): 27–34.

Kadushin, Alfred. *Adopting Older Children.* New York: Columbia University Press, 1970.

Kadushin, Alfred and Seidl, Frederick. "Adoption Failure: A Social Work Postmortem." *Social Work,* vol. 16 (July 1971): 32–37.

Klein, Carol. *The Single Parent Experience.* New York: Avon, 1973.

McNamara, Joan. *The Adoption Adviser.* New York: Hawthorn Books, 1975.

McNamara, Joan, and McNamara, Bernard. *The Special Child Handbook.* New York: Hawthorn Books, 1977.

Peoples, Janet. *Stepping Out: The DeBolts Grow Up* (film). Mill Valley, Calif.: David Productions, 1981.

Rondell, Florence, and Murray, Anne Marie. *New Dimensions in Adoption.* New York: Crown, 1974.

Shyne, Ann, and Schroeder, Anita. *National Study of Social Services to Children and Their Families.* Washington: Department of Health, Education and Welfare, 1978.

Sisto, Grace. "An Agency Designed for Permanency Planning in Foster Care." *Child Welfare,* vol. LIX, no 2 (February 1980): 103–111.

Standards for Adoption Service. Rev. ed. New York: Child Welfare League of America, 1978.

Ward, Margaret. "Parental Bonding in Older-Child Adoptions." *Child Welfare,* vol. LX, no. 1 (January 1981): 24–34.

Who Are the DeBolts? (film). Mill Valley, CA: Korty Film, 1978.

Notes

1. Shyne and Schroeder, 1978.
2. *Adopting,* undated.
3. Peoples, 1981; *Who Are the Debolts?,* 1978.
4. Kadushin and Seidl, 1971.
5. Berman, 1974.
6. Child Welfare League of America, 1978, p. 45.
7. Grow and Shapiro, 1974.
8. Ibid.
9. Sisto, 1980.
10. Goldstein et al., 1973.
11. *City Council President's Adoption Research Project,* 1980.

7. INDEPENDENT ADOPTIONS (pages 69–79)

Sources

Berman, Claire. *We Take This Child: A Candid Look at Modern Adoption.* Garden City, NY: Doubleday, 1974.

Farmer, Robert. *How to Adopt a Child.* New York: Arco, 1967.

McNamara, Joan. *The Adoption Adviser.* New York: Hawthorn Books, 1975.

Meegan, William, et al. "Independent Adoptions." *Child Welfare,* vol. 57, no. 7 (July/August 1978): 450–452.

Ramsey, Judith. "A True-Life Drama: We Paid $10,000 for Our Baby." *Family Circle,* vol. 91, no. 5 (April 1978): 56, 226.

Sorosky, Arthur, et al. *The Adoption Triangle: The Effects of the Sealed Record on Adoptees, Birth Parents, and Adoptive Parents.* Garden City, NY: Anchor Press/Doubleday, 1978.

Notes

1. Farmer, 1967.
2. Meegan et al., 1978.
3. Sorosky et al., 1978.

8. INTERNATIONAL ADOPTIONS (pages 81–96)

Sources

American Public Welfare Association. *Intercountry Adoption Guidelines.* Washington, DC: Department of Health, Education and Welfare, 1980a.

National Directory of Intercountry Adoption Service Resources. Washington: Department of Health, Education and Welfare, 1980b.

Benet, Mary Kathleen. *The Politics of Adoption.* Glencoe, NY: The Free Press, 1976.

Berman, Claire. *We Take This Child: A Candid Look at Modern Adoption.* Garden City, NY: Doubleday, 1974.

Buck, Pearl. *Children for Adoption.* New York: Random House, 1964.

Discussion Papers on Themes Related to the International Year of the Child, Adoption. Geneva: Office of Education of the World Council of Churches, 1979.

McNamara, Joan. *The Adoption Adviser.* New York: Hawthorn Books, 1975.

Nelson-Erichsen, Jean, and Erichsen, Heino. *Gamines: How to Adopt from Latin America.* Minneapolis: Dillon Press, 1981.

———. *How to Adopt from Africa, Asia, Europe and the Pacific Islands.* Minneapolis: Los Niños International Adoption Information Center, 1981.

An Overview to Adopting a Child From Latin America. Issue no. 1. Seaford, NY: Latin America Parents Association, 1980.

Report on Foreign Adoption. Boulder, CO: International Concerns Committee for Children, 1980.

Notes

1. American Public Welfare Association, 1980a.
2. *Discussion Papers on Themes Related to the International Year of the Child, Adoption*, 1979.

9. WAITING FOR YOUR CHILD (pages 97–101)

Sources

Berman, Claire. *We Take This Child: A Candid Look at Modern Adoption.* Garden City, NY: Doubleday, 1974.

Farmer, Robert. *How to Adopt a Child.* New York: Arco, 1967.

Gochros, Harvey. *Not Parents Yet: A Study of the Post Placement Period in Adoption.* Minneapolis: Department of Public Welfare, 1962.

Jewett, Claudia. *Adopting the Older Child.* Harvard: Harvard Common Press, 1978.

McNamara, Joan. *The Adoption Adviser.* New York: Hawthorn Books, 1975.

Raymond, Louise. *Adoption and After.* Rev. ed. New York: Harper & Row, 1974.

Notes

1. Gochros, 1962.

PART III

10. WHAT TO EXPECT (pages 105–112)

Sources

Anderson, David. *Children of Special Value: Interracial Adoption in America.* New York: St. Martin's Press, 1971.

Chess, Stella. *An Introduction to Child Psychiatry.* 2d ed. New York: Grune and Stratton, 1969.

Elonen, Anna, and Schwartz, Edward. "A Longitudinal Study of Emotional, Social, and Academic Functioning of Adopted Children." *Child Welfare,* vol. XLVIII, no. 2 (February 1969): 72–78.

Farber, Susan. "Telltale Behavior of Twins." *Psychology Today* (January 1981): 59–62, 79–80.

Gardner, Richard. *Understanding Children.* New York: Jason Aronson, 1973.

Gochros, Harvey. *Not Parents Yet: A Study of the Post Placement Period in Adoption.* Minneapolis: Department of Public Welfare, 1962.

Hammons, Chloe. "The Adoptive Family." *American Journal of Nursing*, vol. 76, no. 2 (February 1976): 251–257.

Jaffee, Benson, and Fanshel, David. *How They Fared in Adoption: A Follow-Up Study*. New York: Columbia University Press, 1970.

Kadushin, Alfred. *Adopting Older Children*. New York: Columbia University Press, 1970.

Kirk, David. *Shared Fate*. Glencoe, NY: The Free Press, 1964.

Kornitzer, Margaret. *Adoption and Family Life*. New York: Humanities Press, 1968.

Krugman, Dorothy. "Reality in Adoption." *Child Welfare* (July 1964): 349–358.

McWhinnie, Alexina. "The Adopted Child in Adolescence." In G. Caplan and S. Lebovici, eds., *Adolescence*. New York: Basic Books, 1969.

———. *Adopted Children: How They Grow Up*. London: Routledge & Kegan Paul, 1967.

Raymond, Louise. *Adoption and After*. Rev. ed. New York: Harper & Row, 1974.

Seglow, Jean, et al. *Growing Up Adopted*. Windsor: National Foundation for Education and Research in England and Wales, 1972.

Sorosky, Arthur, et al. *The Adoption Triangle*. Garden City, NY: Anchor Press/Doubleday, 1978.

Thomas, Alexander, et al. *Temperament and Behavior Disorders in Children*. New York: University Press, 1968.

Thomas, Alexander, and Chess, Stella. *Temperament and Development*. New York: Brunner/Mazel, 1977.

Triseliotis, John. *In Search of Origins*. London: Routledge & Kegan Paul, 1973.

Zur Nieden, Margaret. "The Influence of Constitution and Environment Upon the Development of Adopted Children." *Journal of Psychology*, vol. 31 (1951): 91–95.

Notes

1. Kirk, 1964, p. 50.
2. Chess, 1969, p. 36.
3. Sorosky et al., 1978.

4. Anderson, 1971; McWhinnie, 1967.
5. Jaffee and Fanshel, 1970; Thomas et al., 1968; Thomas and Chess, 1977.
6. Thomas et al., 1968.
7. Raymond, 1974.
8. McWhinnie, 1969; Triseliotis, 1973.
9. Chess, 1969, p. 96.
10. Kirk, 1964, p. 160.

11. TELLING YOUR CHILD ABOUT ADOPTION (pages 113–122)

Sources

Anderson, David. *Children of Special Value: Interracial Adoption in America*. New York: St. Martin's Press, 1971.

Buck, Pearl. *Children for Adoption*. New York: Random House, 1964.

Carney, Ann. *No More Here and There: Adopting the Older Child.* Chapel Hill: University of North Carolina Press, 1976.

Elonen, Anna, and Schwartz, Edward. "A Longitudinal Study of Emotional, Social and Academic Functioning of Adopted Children." *Child Welfare*, vol. XLVIII, no. 2 (February 1969): 72–78.

Glenn, Jules. "The Adoption Theme in Edward Albee's Tiny Alice and the American Dream." *Psychoanalytic Study of the Child*, vol. 29 (1974): 413–429.

Jaffee, Benson, and Fanshel, David. *How They Fared in Adoption: A Follow-Up Study*. New York: Columbia University Press, 1970.

Kirk, David. *Shared Fate*. Glencoe, NY: The Free Press, 1964.

Kornitzer, Margaret. *Adoption and Family Life*. New York: Humanities Press, 1968.

Krugman, Dorothy. "Reality in Adoption." *Child Welfare* (July 1964): 349–358.

McNamara, Joan. *The Adoption Adviser*. New York: Hawthorn Books, 1975.

McWhinnie, Alexina. *Adopted Children: How They Grow Up*. London: Routledge & Kegan Paul, 1967.

Raymond, Louise. *Adoption and After*. Rev. ed. New York: Harper & Row, 1974.

Sorosky, Arthur, et al. *The Adoption Triangle: The Effect of the Sealed Record on Adoptees, Birth Parents and Adoptive Parents.* Garden City, NY: Anchor Press/Doubleday, 1978.

Triseliotis, John. *In Search of Origins: The Experiences of Adopted People.* London: Routledge & Kegan Paul, 1973.

Notes

1. Buck, 1964, p. 211.
2. Elonen and Schwartz, 1969; Jaffee and Fanshel, 1970; Kornitzer, 1968; McWhinnie, 1967; Triseliotis, 1973.
3. Elonen and Schwartz, 1969.
4. McWhinnie, 1967; Triseliotis, 1973.
5. Kornitzer, 1968; Sorosky et al., 1978.
6. Kornitzer, 1968.
7. McNamara, 1975, p. 153.
8. Buck, 1964, p. 211.
9. Raymond, 1974.

12. SEARCHING FOR ORIGINS (pages 123–132)

Sources

Carney, Ann. *No More Here and There: Adopting the Older Child.* Chapel Hill: University of North Carolina Press, 1976.

Eiduson, Bernice, and Livermore, Jean. "Complications in Therapy With Adopted Children." *The American Journal of Orthopsychiatry,* vol. 23 (October 1953): 795–802.

Erickson, Erik. *Identity: Youth and Crises.* New York: W. W. Norton, 1968.

———. *Life History and the Historical Moment.* New York: W. W. Norton, 1975.

Fisher, Florence. *In Search of Anna Fisher.* Greenwich, CT: Fawcett Publications, 1973.

Jaffee, Benson, and Fanshel, David. *How They Fared in Adoption: A Follow-Up Study.* New York: Columbia University Press, 1970.

Kornitzer, Margaret. *Adoption and Family Life.* New York: Humanities Press, 1968.

Lifton, Betty Jean. *Twice Born: Memoirs of an Adopted Daughter.* New York: McGraw-Hill, 1975.

McWhinnie, Alexina. *Adopted Children: How They Grow Up*. London: Routledge & Kegan Paul, 1967.

Sorosky, Arthur, et al. *The Adoption Triangle: The Effect of the Sealed Record on Adoptees, Birth Parents and Adoptive Parents*. Garden City, NY: Anchor Press/Doubleday, 1978.

Triseliotis, John. *In Search of Origins: The Experiences of Adopted People*. London: Routledge & Kegan Paul, 1973.

Notes

1. Fisher, 1973; Sorosky et al., 1978.
2. Triseliotis, 1973.
3. Ibid.
4. Lifton, 1975, p. 94.
5. Ibid.
6. Carney, 1976, p. 46.
7. Jaffee and Fanshel, 1970; Triseliotis, 1973.
8. Sorosky et al., 1978.
9. Lifton, 1975.
10. Sorosky, 1978.
11. Fisher, 1973; Sorosky et al., 1978; Triseliotis, 1973.
12. Sorosky et al., 1978.
13. Ibid.
14. Ibid.
15. Ibid.
16. Sorosky et al., 1978; Triseliotis, 1973.
17. Sorosky et al., 1978.
18. Ibid.
19. Sorosky et al., 1978; Triseliotis, 1973.
20. Triseliotis, 1973.
21. Fisher, 1973; Sorosky et al., 1978; Triseliotis, 1973.

13. HANDLING UPSETTING REMARKS (pages 133–141)

Sources

Blank, Joseph. *Nineteen Steps Up the Mountain: The Story of the DeBolt Family*. New York: Lippincott, 1976.

Grow, Lucille, and Shapiro, Deborah. *Black Children White Parents: A Study of Transracial Adoption*. New York: Child Welfare League, 1974.

Kadushin, Alfred. *Adopting Older Children*. New York: Columbia University Press, 1970.

Kirk, David. *Shared Fate.* New York: The Free Press, 1964.

Klibanoff, Susan, and Klibanoff, Elton. *Let's Talk About Adoption.* Boston: Little, Brown, 1973.

Kornitzer, Margaret. *Adoption and Family Life.* New York: Humanities Press, 1968.

McNamara, Joan. *The Adoption Adviser.* New York: Hawthorn Books, 1975.

Raymond, Louise. *Adoption and After.* Rev. ed. New York: Harper & Row, 1974.

Rondell, Florence, and Murray Anne-Marie. *New Dimensions in Adoption.* New York: Crown, 1974.

Sorosky, Arthur, et al. *The Adoption Triangle: The Effect of the Sealed Record on Adoptees, Birth Parents and Adoptive Parents.* Garden City, NY: Anchor Press/Doubleday, 1978.

Triseliotis, John. *In Search of Origins: The Experiences of Adopted People.* London: Routledge & Kegan Paul, 1973.

Notes

1. Kirk, 1964.
2. Kornitzer, 1968; Sorosky et al.
3. Blank, 1976.
4. Grow and Shapiro, 1974.
5. Kirk, 1964.
6. Ibid.
7. Rondell and Murray, 1974.
8. Kadushin, 1970.
9. Kirk, 1964.

14. OVERCOMING PROBLEMS (pages 143–151)

Sources

Anderson, David. *Children of Special Value: Interracial Adoption in America.* New York: St. Martin's Press, 1971.

Carney, Ann. *No More Here and There: Adopting the Older Child.* Chapel Hill: University of North Carolina Press, 1976.

Elonen, Anna, and Schwartz, Edward. "A Longitudinal Study of Emotional, Social and Academic Functioning of Adopted Children." *Child Welfare,* vol. XLVIII, no. 2 (February 1969): 72–78.

Gardner, Richard. *Understanding Children.* New York: Jason Aronson, 1973.

Gesell, Arnold, et al. *The Child from Five to Ten.* New York: Harper & Row, 1974.

Gesell, Arnold, et al. *Youth: The Years from Ten to Sixteen.* New York: Harper & Row, 1956.

Glenn, Jules. "The Adoption Themes in Edward Albee's Tiny Alice and the American Dream." *Psychoanalytic Study of the Child,* vol. 29 (1974): 413–429.

Ilg, Frances, and Ames, Louise. *Child Behavior.* New York: Perennial Library, 1955.

Kirk, David, et al. "Are Adopted Children Especially Vulnerable to Stress?" *Archive of General Psychiatry,* vol. 14 (March 1966): 291.

Klibanoff, Susan, and Klibanoff, Elton. *Let's Talk About Adoption.* Boston: Little, Brown, 1973.

McNamara, Joan. *The Adoption Adviser.* New York: Hawthorn Books, 1975.

McWhinnie, Alexina. *Adopted Children: How They Grow Up.* London: Routledge & Kegan Paul, 1967.

McWhinnie, Alexina. "The Adopted Child in Adolescence." *Adolescence.* Edited by Caplan and Lebovici. New York: Basic Books, 1969.

Pine, Maya. "Only Isn't Lonely (Or Spoiled or Selfish)." *Psychology Today,* vol. 15, no. 3 (March 1981): 15–19.

Raymond, Louise. *Adoption and After.* Rev. ed. New York: Harper & Row, 1974.

Rondell, Florence, and Murray, Anne-Marie. *New Dimensions in Adoption.* New York: Crown, 1974.

Sorosky, Arthur, et al. *The Adoption Triangle.* Garden City, NY: Anchor Press/Doubleday, 1978.

Spock, Benjamin. *Baby and Child Care.* New York: Pocket Book, 1968.

Thomas, Alexander, et al. *Temperament and Behavior Disorders in Children.* New York: New York University Press, 1968.

Thomas, Alexander, and Chess, Stella. *Temperament and Development.* New York: Brunner/Mazel, 1977.

Wallerstein, Judith, and Kelly, Joan. "California's Children of Divorce." *Psychology Today*, vol. 13, no. 8 (January 1980): 67–76.

Zur Nieden, Margaret. "The Influence of Constitution and Environment Upon the Development of Adopted Children." *Journal of Psychology*, vol. 31 (1951): 91–95.

Notes

1. Elonen and Schwartz, 1969, p. 78.
2. Sorosky et al., 1978, p. 78.
3. Ilg and Ames, 1955.
4. Elonen and Schwartz, 1969, Kirk, et al., 1966.
5. Elonen and Schwartz, 1969.
6. Pine, 1981.
7. Elonen and Schwartz, 1969.
8. Wallerstein and Kelly, 1980.

PART IV

15. CHANGING THE SYSTEM (pages 155–176)

Sources

Benet, Mary Kathleen. *The Politics of Adoption*. Glencoe, NY: The Free Press, 1976.

Barbour, John. "Three Generations of Women, Three Lifestyles." *St. Petersberg Times*, June 3, 1979, pp. 1A, 12A.

Boyne, John. *Financial Forces in the Adoption of "Hard to Place" Children*. Testimony to the National Commission for Children in Need of Parents, Philadelphia, Pennsylvania, January 26, 1978.

Bureau of the Census. *Statistical Abstract of the United States*. Washington, DC: U.S. Government Printing Office, 1980.

City Council President's Adoption Research Project. New York: The City of New York, 1980.

Darabi, Katherine, et al. "The Second Time Around: Birth Spacing Among Teenage Mothers." In Irving Stuart and Carl Wells, eds., *The Pregnant Adolescent: Needs, Problems and Management*. New York: Van Nostrand Reinhold, 1981.

"D.C. Foster Care: Wards of the Bureaucracy." *Adoptalk*, vol. 6, no. 6 (July 1981): 4.

Duncan, Sydney. "Finding Homes for Black Children." Address to the Sun Coast Council on Adoptable Children, Largo, Florida, February 17, 1980.

Fanshel, David."Children Discharged From Foster Care." *Child Welfare*, vol. LVIII, no. 8 (September/October 1978): 467–483.

———. "Pre-schoolers Entering Foster Care: The Need to Stress Plans for Permanency." *Child Welfare*, vol. LVIII, no. 2 (February 1979): 67–87.

Finch, Gerald, and Bronston, David. *Good Money After Bad: An Analysis of Expenditures and Performance in Private-Sector Foster Care*. New York: Office of the City Council President, 1979.

Goldstein, Joseph, et al. *Beyond the Best Interest of the Child*. Glencoe, NY: The Free Press, 1973.

Hill, Robert. *The Strengths of Black Families*. New York: Emerson Hall, 1971.

Kornitzer, Margaret. *Adoption and Family Life*. New York: Humanities Press, 1968.

Martin, Katherine. *Teenage Pregnancy: A Discussion of the Problem*. White Plains, NY: Department of Social Services, 1979.

McWhinnie, Alexina. "The Adopted Child in Adolescence." In Caplan and Lebovici, eds. *Adolescence*. New York: Basic Books, 1969.

National Center for Social Statistics. *Monthly Vital Statistics Report*. Vol. 30, no. 6 (September 29, 1981).

"1980 Child Welfare Law Funded at $163.5 Million." *Adoptalk*, vol. 6, no. 1 (December 1980/January 1981): 1–2.

Philliber, Susan, et al. "Coping With Adolescent Pregnancy." In Paul Ahmed, ed., *Coping With Pregnancy*. New York: Elsevier-North Holland, 1980.

Philliber, Susan and Rothenberg, Pearilla. *The Impact of Single Parenthood on Mothers and Their Children*. New York: Center for Population and Family Health, Columbia University, 1980.

Schaffer, Judith, et al. *Compendium of Research on Foster Care in New York City*. New York: Office of the City Council President, 1979.

Seglow, Jean, et al. *Growing Up Adopted*. Windsor: The National Foundation for Educational Research in England and Wales, 1972.

Shyne, Ann. "Who Are the Children? A National Overview of Services." *Social Work Research and Abstracts*, vol. 16, no. 1 (Spring 1980): 26–33.

Sisto, Grace. "An Agency Designed for Permanency Planning in Foster Care." *Child Welfare*, vol. LIX, no. 2 (February 1980): 103–111.

Sorosky, Arthur, et al. *The Adoption Triangle*. Garden City, NY: Anchor Press/Doubleday, 1978.

Steketee, John. "Concern for Children in Placement." *Adoption Report*, vol. 3, no. 2 (Spring 1978): 2.

Sung, Kyu-Taik, and Rothrock, Dorothy. "An Alternate School for Pregnant Teenagers and Teenage Mothers." *Child Welfare*, vol. LIX, no. 7 (July/August 1980): 427–434.

Teenage Pregnancy: A Report to Governor Hugh L. Carey. Albany: New York State Department of Social Services, 1978.

Teenage Pregnancy: The Problem That Hasn't Gone Away. New York: The Alan Guttmacher Institute, 1981.

Tremitiere, Barbara. *Model Placement Services for Children with Special Needs: The "Client-Centered" Approach*. York, PA: Tressler-Lutheran Service Associates, 1980.

Triseliotis, John. *In Search of Origins: The Experience of Adopted People*. London: Routledge & Kegan Paul, 1973.

Young, David, and Allen, Brandt. "Cost Benefit Analysis in the Social Services: The Example of Adoption Reimbursement." *Social Service Review* (June 1977): 249–264.

Notes

1. Seglow et al., 1972, p. 161.
2. Bureau of the Census, 1980; National Center for Social Statistics, 1977.
3. *Teenage Pregnancy*, 1981.
4. Ibid.
5. Ibid.
6. Ibid.
7. Ibid.
8. Shyne, 1980.
9. *Teenage Pregnancy*, 1978.
10. Sisto, 1980.
11. *Teenage Pregnancy*, 1978.
12. *Teenage Pregnancy*, 1981.
13 Martin, 1979.

14. Ibid.
15. Fanshel, 1979.
16. "D.C. Foster Care . . . ", 1981; Steketee, 1978.
17. *City Council President's Adoption Research Project*, 1980.
18. Ibid.
19. Goldstein, et al., 1978.
20. Tremitiere, 1980.
21. Ibid.
22. Hill, 1971.
23. Duncan, 1981.
24. Ibid., 1977.
25. Young, 1977.
26. Sisto, 1980.
27. McWhinnie, 1969.
28. Sorosky, 1978; Triseliotis, 1973.

Index